ADVENT

of

THE ARYANS

in

INDIA

ADVENT *of* THE ARYANS *in* INDIA

RAM SHARAN SHARMA

MANOHAR
2026

First published 1999
Reprinted 2026

ISBN 978-81-7304-289-8

Published by
Ajay Kumar Jain *for*
Manohar Publishers & Distributors
4753/23 Ansari Road, Daryaganj
New Delhi 110 002

Printed and bound in India

Contents

Maps

Preface

My *Looking for the Aryans* (1995) deals with the when and where of the characteristics of the Aryan culture. The present publication discusses the archaeology of the early Vedic culture known from textual and lexical data. It uses the results of recent diggings to point out the features of the pastoral life of Central Asia in the early second millennium BC, and to indicate the movements of the horse-using tribes to the Indian subcontinent. The study also examines the question of the presence of pre-Aryan languages and the diffusion of the Indo-Aryan language in the subcontinent.

The book has grown out of a paper that I wrote at the instance of Professor Rajesh Kochar. In preparing its script I have taken help from Gunakar Mule, Professor Anjani Kumar Sinha, Dr Sitaram Roy, Dr Angraj Chaudhary, Dr Basudev Narain, Dr Anjani Kumar and Dr Mrityunjay Kumar. To all of them my sincere thanks.

I would also like to express my gratitude to M.S. Andronov, A.H. Dani, Kent H. Gordon and Kenneth L. Pike, J. Harmatta, J.P. Mallory, and Alexander Mongait, whose works I have used in preparing the maps. I also thank M. Yasin (Cartolabs) and Bachi Ram for cartographic help.

Patna R.S. SHARMA
25 September 1998

Introduction

The term 'Aryan' was especially applied to those who spoke Vedic and Avestan languages, but gradually speakers of all Indo-European languages came to be called Aryan. The Aryan question has been debated for nearly two hundred years. There are more than a dozen theories about the original home of the Aryans or the Indo-Europeans and many views about the routes they took out of their homeland. These findings are conditioned by time, place, and political and intellectual climate. Some authors underline the racial and linguistic homogeneity of the Aryans, but others question this conclusion and expose the racial myth.[1] However, despite their shortcomings the contributions of the earlier scholars cannot be discarded. Interest in the Aryan problem and the needs of the Christian missionaries led to the publication of *A Sanskrit-English Dictionary* by Monier Monier-Williams in 1872. This publication continues to be an invaluable reference work partly because it was the first book of an English scholar to discover cognates for Sanskrit

[1]Kenneth A.R. Kennedy, 'Have Aryans been identified in the prehistoric skeletal record from South Asia? Biological anthropology and concepts of ancient races', in George Erdosy, ed. *The Indo-Aryans of Ancient South Asia*, Munshiram Manoharlal, New Delhi, 1997, pp. 32-66; Thomas R. Trautmann, *Aryans and British India*, Vistaar Publication, New Delhi, 1997.

words in the eastern and western branches of the Indo-European language.

During the last hundred years or so the 'Aryan' subject has been growing, and several of the old theories have been modified, altered and superseded. This has happened with a scholar like Max Müller. In the initial stage he identified the Indo-European language with an Indo-European race, but in 1888 he questioned the theory that the speakers of the Indo-European languages belonged to the same race.[2] There is no doubt that Indo-European scholarship has enriched linguistics and ancient history, but there is still scope for research and reconstruction. In India recently the Aryan debate has been vitiated by extra-academic considerations. Some Hindu fundamentalists assert that the Aryans were the original inhabitants of India and created the Harappan culture.[3] The writings of some Western archaeologists who appear to be strong pro-cessualists encourage this type of thinking. The validity of the fundamentalist view can be better tested if aspects of the Aryan culture are analysed in a wider horizon and not confined to the Indian perspective. More importantly, we have to ask whether cultural traits known from textual, lexical and linguistic data fit the archaeological reality.

[2]*Biographies of Words and the Home of the Aryans*, London, 1888.

[3]K.D. Sethna, *The Problem of Aryan Origin from an Indian Perspective*, S. & S. Publishers, Calcutta, 1980; A.K. Biswas, 'The Aryan Myth', in A. Ray and B. Mukherji, eds., *Historical Archaeology*, Books & Books, New Delhi, 1990, pp. 30-59

CHAPTER 1

Markers of the Aryan Culture

The main traits of the Aryan culture can be determined on the basis of the Vedic, Iranian and Greek literary texts and cognate terms found in the Proto-Indo-European languages. The texts which help us to reconstruct the material and other aspects of the Aryan culture consist of the *Rg Veda*, the *Zend-Avesta* and Homer's *Iliad* and *Odyssey*. Specialists may differ on the criteria for dating these texts, but we may go by the generally accepted dates. The first is assigned roughly to 1500 BC, although its later strata might be as late as 1000 BC. The second is roughly attributed to 1400 BC, and the Greek epics to 900-800 BC. These texts do not represent historical accounts in the sense we understand them, but can certainly be used as sources. Although they belong to different regions, they suggest a period when copper and bronze were in use. The later portions of Homer mention iron. However, bronze does not play any vital role in the life of the people. Generally the texts represent agriculture and pastoralism as the main sources of livelihood. A study of these texts together with that of cognate words in early Indo-European languages suggests certain distinctive features of the Aryan life. The people lived in a temperate climate. They domesticated horses which were used for riding and driving carts. Some texts specify that they used spoked wheels, and fought with bows and arrows placed in quivers. They lived in a male-dominated society. They buried the dead but also practised cremation. The cults of fire and *soma* prevailed among the speakers of the Indo-European languages in Iran and the Indian subcontinent. However, animal sacrifice and horse sacrifice seem to have obtained among all Indo-European communities. The most important mark of the Aryan culture is its language.

Where and in what stage of archaeological culture should we look for these traits? The cultural contents of the texts belong roughly to the late Neolithic and early Bronze Ages. As regards the area, we may consider Eastern Europe and Central Asia, which are geographically linked to India, Pakistan, Afghanistan, Iran, Iraq, Anatolia and Greece. In a major portion of this vast territory in ancient times various communities spoke Indo-European languages. Climatic conditions, environment, birds, animals and trees revealed by the cognate words rule out the choice of warmer areas, and our search has to be confined to Eastern Europe and Central Asia.

The horse, its domestication and diffusion

The horse is regarded as an indispensable marker of the Aryan culture, and it plays a crucial role in the life of the early Indo-Europeans. The term *aśva* and its cognates appear in Sanskrit, Avestan, Greek, Latin and other Indo-European languages. In ancient texts, particularly in Vedic and Avestan, many personal names are horse-centred. For the Vedic period before 1000 BC we have over 50 horse names and thirty chariot names.[1] Some Iranian

[1]Morton Smith, 'What is in a name (in ancient India)?', *Journal of Indo-European Studies* (*JIES*), 12, 1984, p. 306.

tribes mentioned by Herodotus are named after the horse, and the Kassites, who invaded Babylonia in the beginning of the sixteenth century BC, seem to have a horse-based tribal name. In its various forms the term *aśva* occurs 215 times in the *Ṛg Veda*; no other animal is mentioned so frequently. The term *go* occurs 176 times and *vṛṣabha* 170 times. These two terms suggest the importance of cattle rearing. However, cattle rearers were dominated by a horse-based aristocracy. The tiger and rhinoceros, typical of the tropical and semitropical climate of India, were rare in the cold conditions of Central Asia. They do not find mention in the *Rg Veda*, and similar other animals of the tropical and semitropical zone such as the lion, deer, buffalo and elephant do not appear so much in this text, as the horse, cow and bull. This difference suggests Central Asian influence on the animal world of the *Rg Veda*.

The horse is praised in two complete hymns of the *Rg Veda*.[2] Almost all the Vedic gods are associated with it, and this specially applies to Indra and his companions the Maruts. Though the Vedic people frequently pray for *prajā* and *paśu*, they also specifically ask for horses, sometimes as many as a thousand. In the *Avesta* cattle wealth seems to be more important, but the horse has its own importance. Both the horse and the chariot repeatedly occur in prayers made to Mithra.[3] The sun is always described as swift-horsed or one possessing swift horses.[4] Much later, the seven-horse chariot of the sun became

[2] I. 61-2.

[3] *The Zend Avesta*, pt II, tr. James Darmesteter, *Sacred Books of the East* (SBE), XXIII, rpt, Motilal Banarsidass, Delhi, 1988, pp. 136, 138, 152, 157.

[4] Ibid., pp. 142, 350-1; XXXI, pp. 256, 271.

widely known in Indian iconography. The adjective 'swift-horsed' is also applied in the *Avesta* to another divinity called Apām-Napāt,[5] who is also a Vedic deity. Zoroaster blesses the young King Vistaspa with wealth in horses and prays to the gods to bestow on him swift horses and good strong sons.[6] Significantly enough, as in the name of Vistaspa, *aspa* or 'horse' forms a part of the names of several chiefs or warriors such as Pourusaspa (the father of Zoroaster), Karesaspa, Gushtaspa and Gamaspa.[7] The horse formed such an integral part of the life of the ruling segment in Iran that the penalty for offences, religious or mundane, was administered with a horse goad (*asphe-astra*) or stripe.[8] Though references to the horse are few in the Gāthās, the earliest portion of the *Avesta*, only a few fragments form this portion of the larger text, which itself is incomplete.[9] However, as a whole, the *Avesta* is familiar with the horse in general[10] and also with the chariot horse[11] and the saddle horse[12] in particular. The horse and the horse-drawn chariot are equally important in Homer.[13] The equerry or officer in charge of the horse of the chief is commonly mentioned in the *Odyssey*.[14] Therefore the Vedic,

[5]Ibid., XXI, p. 219.

[6]Ibid., XXIII, pp. 328, 340.

[7]Ibid., pp. 324-9; cf. XXXI, pp. 235, 247 with fn. 49, p. 250

[8]*SBE*, IV, *The Zend Avesta*, pt I, Introduction, p. XCVI, p. 31.

[9]Ibid., XXXI, pp. 120, 173-4.

[10]Ibid., pp. 173, 199, 204, 216, 270-1, 276.

[11]Ibid., XXIII, pp. 136, 138.

[12]Ibid., p. 124 with fn. 3.

[13]*The Iliad*, tr. E.V. Rieu, Penguin, Harmondsworth, rpt, 1986, Bk. XXIII, pp. 412-19.

[14]*The Odyssey*, tr. E.V. Rieu, Penguin, Harmondsworth, rpt, 1986, Bk. VIII, p. 125.

Iranian and Greek texts make it clear that the earliest speakers of Indo-European languages were very well acquainted with the horse. This is confirmed by some West Asian inscriptions of the second millennium BC.

The earliest domesticated horse is found at a considerable distance from the Indian subcontinent. It is significant that the largest number of horses appear in the area between the Dnieper river in the west and the Volga river in the east. Archaeologically the horse first appears in the south Ural region around 6000 BC.[15] According to Marija Gimbutas the sheep herders of the Volga steppe were probably 'the first to domesticate the horse'[16] although its remains are also reported in the Black Sea region around the sixth millennium BC. In the fourth millennium BC the horse appears in Anatolia (modern Turkey) south of the Black Sea. By the third millennium BC horses appear in large numbers in south Siberia. Though there is an ideogram for horse in the Elamite script in south-eastern Iran in the beginning of the third millennium BC, and also in the Sumerian script in 2500 BC,[17] this animal does not play any important role in the life of Western Asia in the fourth and the first half of the third millennia BC. However, it seems

[15]'Comments' by Marija Gimbutas on David A. Anthony, 'The "Kurgan culture", Indo-European Origins, and the domestication of the horse: A reconsideration', *Current Anthropology*, vol. 27, no. 4, Aug.-Oct. 1986, p. 306; G. Matyushin, 1986, quoted in M. Zvelebil and K.V. Zvelebil, 'Agricultural transition and Indo-European dispersals', *Antiquity*, vol. 62, no. 236, Sept. 1988, p. 581.

[16]*Current Anthropology*, vol. 27, 1986, p. 306.

[17]I.M. Diakonov, 'On the original home of the speakers of Indo-European', *Journal of Indo-European Studies*, vol. 13, 1985, p. 168 fn. 2.

to have been known in Iran at Sialk III[18] and in Mundigak[19] in southern Afghanistan. Evidently the use of the horse underwent a long gestation period. Although it was known around 6000 BC in the area between the Black Sea and the south Urals, it came into general use in Eurasia only around 2000 BC.

There is no doubt that in the initial stage this animal was used on a considerable scale by the speakers of the Proto-Iranian or Proto-Indian language. It is significant that the terms connected with *aśva* or horse appear in hieroglyphic Hittite, in Hebrew, Akkadian and the Caucasian languages.[20] The term for a horse trainer present in the Assyrian records in the second millennium BC is traced to an Indo-European etymology.[21] Clearly, the speakers of the Aryan language used the horse and spread it through Western Asia.

The earliest inscriptional evidence for the use of the horse on some scale in Western Asia belongs to the second half of the nineteenth century BC. We learn that mounted horses were deployed to put down brigands in the countryside of Iraq bordering on Syria. Whether this was done by the Kassites is not clear. But the effective advent of the horse in this area is ascribed to the Kassite invasion of Babylonia in 1595 BC. When the horse appeared in this country, it was called the ass of the mountain.

[18]A.H. Dani and V.M. Masson, eds., *History of Civilization of Central Asia*, I, UNESCO Publishing, Paris, 1992, p. 191.

[19]Ibid., p. 217.

[20]J. Harmatta in Dani and Masson, op. cit., pp. 369, 372.

[21]Sarva Daman Singh, *Ancient Indian Warfare with Special Reference to the Vedic Period*, E.J. Brill, Leiden, 1965, pp. 55-6.

The war chariot

The Indo-Europeans widely used horse-drawn chariots which are well known to Vedic, Avestan and Homeric texts. The chariot race prescribed in the *vājapeya* sacrifice of the later Vedic texts was also a Greek practice[22] which is fully described by Homer.[23] There are two words for the chariot in the Proto-Indo-European language, each used in half a dozen of the Indo-European languages. This also applies to the different parts of the chariot. The terms axle, harness and navel (nave) have cognate words in six Indo-European languages. We have also a verbal expression for riding in many Indo-European languages;[24] another cognate verbal expression in Hittite and Sanskrit connotes the yoking of the chariot. There are two separate words for wheel/wagon in the Proto-Indo-European language.[25] One of them may have been adopted by the Indo-Europeans from the Near East through trade and other contacts, but it was made such an integral part of the steppe life that it appears in several Indo-European languages. It is held that the wheeled chariot originated in Western Asia in the fourth millennium BC and reached the steppes of south Russia about the same time.

Sufficient evidence for the presence of the chariot from 3000 BC onwards appears in the excavations of south Russia. Chariots with two or three wheels have been found dating to the third millennium BC. Evidence

[22]R.S. Sharma, *Aspects of Political Ideas and Institutions in Ancient India*, 4th edn, Motilal Banarsidass, Delhi, 1996, pp. 165-6.

[23]*The Iliad*, Bk. XXIII, pp. 419-21.

[24]J.P. Mallory, *In Search of the Indo-Europeans Language, Archaeology and Myth*, Thames and Hudson, London, 1991, p. 274 fn. 20.1, pp. 275-6 fn. 25.

[25]Ibid., pp. 274-5 fn. 25

regarding the presence of horse-drawn chariots appears in the names of the Mitanni rulers around 1400 BC and later. These names mean 'having running chariots', 'facing the chariots', and 'having big horses'. We also hear of the Indo-Iranian title 'horse-driver'.[26] Daśaratha, the name of a Mitanni king, means a person possessing ten chariots. Wooden wheels are known outside India, but until 2000 BC they were generally solidly built. Clay wheels are reported in the Harappan context, but their dates are uncertain; they cannot be earlier than 2500 BC.

Spoked wheels

Spoked wheels appear in Hissar, in Iran and in the north Caucasus area around 2300 BC.[27] A six-spoked wheeled chariot appears on a cylinder seal attributed to Hissar IIIb around 1800 BC.[28] It is said that in the nineteenth century BC the Hittites used light-wheeled chariots to conquer Anatolia. As will be shown later, war chariots with spoked wheels appear around 1700 BC in the Sintashta region in the south Ural area adjoining western Kazakhstan. By 1500 BC spoked wheels appear at several places in Eastern Europe and Western Asia.

There is no evidence for a spoked wheel at Harappa or Mohenjodaro where all the toy-carts found so

[26]Y.Y. Kuzmina and K.F. Smirnov, 'The Origin of the Indo-Iranians in the Light of Recent Archaeological Data', *Journal of Central Asia*, vol. I, no. 1, 1978, p. 69.

[27]David W. Anthony and Bernard Wales, *Current Anthropology*, vol. 29, no. 3, June 1988, p. 443.

[28]Robert H. Dyson, Jr., 'The Archaeological Evidence of the Second Millennium B.C. on the Persian Plateau', *The Cambridge Ancient History*, vol. II, Chap. XVI, revd edn, Cambridge University Press, Bentley House, London, 1968, p. 5.

far have solid wheels.[29] Banawali in Hissar district in Haryana is associated with the use of the spoked wheels in the Harappan phase. According to its excavator, R.S. Bisht, a shard depicts a canopied cart with spoked wheels.[30] But the painted shard produced by him shows seventeen parallel lines[31] which appear to be decorative. These lines cannot be considered spokes, for neither they converge at a hub/central point nor do the distances between them tend to narrow down towards any end. Further, since the calibrated dates for the Harappan phase of Banawali range from 2425 to 1250 BC,[32] it is difficult to fix the date of this shard.

Suraj Bhan speaks of the discovery of a fragmentary disc painted with black converging strokes representing spokes from Mitathal in the same district of the same state, and the disc is dated around 1800 BC.[33] But the strokes shown on Plate XXI[34] of his publication could be decorative designs which do not appear on a wheel. Even if the disc is taken as a wheel, the strokes may

[29]R.E.M. Wheeler, *The Indus Civilization*, 3rd edn, Cambridge University Press, Bentley House, London, 1968, pp. 82, 92; Iravatham Mahadevan, 'Study of the Indus Script through Bi-lingual Parallels', in Gregory L. Possehl, ed., *Ancient Cities of the Indus*, Vikas Publishing House, New Delhi, 1979, p. 264.

[30]R.S. Bisht, 'Excavations at Banawali: 1974-77', in Gregory L. Possehl, ed., *Harappan Civilization: A Contemporary Perspective*, Oxford and IBH, New Delhi, 1982, pp. 113-39.

[31]Ibid., Plate 10.7 on p. 128.

[32]Jim G. Shaffer, 'The Indus Valley, Baluchistan and Helmand Traditions: Neolithic through Bronze Age', in Robert W. Ehrich, ed., *Chronologies in Old World Archaeology*, vol. I, 3rd edn, University of Chicago Press, Chicago, 1992, p. 433.

[33]Suraj Bhan, *Excavation at Mitathal (1968) and Other Explorations in the Sutlej-Yamuna Divide*, Kurukshetra University, Kurukshetra, 1975, pp. 68-70.

[34]Ibid.

indicate the joinings of the wooden planks used in making it. The spoked wheel, if really present, may have been adopted around 1500 BC because of contact with the Indo-Aryans.

In the second millennium BC remains of the horse appear in south Central Asia, Iran and Afghanistan. By around 1500 BC representations of the horse and the chariot are found in Kirgizia, the Altai zone, Mangolia, the Pamir mountain ranges and, above all, in south Tajikistan.[35]

Horse remains in South Asia

In the third millennium BC only a few horse remains have been identified in the Indian subcontinent, and even they are of a doubtful nature. Richard Meadow, who has made a thorough study of the remains, finds no clear osteological evidence of the presence of the horse in the Indian subcontinent until 2000 BC. In his view the Pirak complex located near the Bolan pass in the Kachi plains of Baluchistan provides the earliest evidence of the true horse in South Asia.[36] This view is also held by Shaffer, who

[35]Asko Parpola, 'The Coming of the Aryans to Iran and India and the Cultural and Ethnic Identity of the Dāsas', *International Journal of Dravidian Linguistics,* XVII, no. 2, p. 143; cf. Henri-Paul Frankfort, 'New data illustrating the early contacts between Central Asia and the North West of the Sub-Continent', in Catherine Jarrige, ed., *South Asian Archaeology,* 1989, Prehistory Press, Madison, 1992, p. 99.

[36]Richard Meadow, 'Continuity and Change in the agriculture of the Great Indus Valley: The palaeoethnobotanical and zooarchaeological evidence', in J.M. Kenoyer, ed., *Old Problems and New Perspective of the Archaeology of South Asia,* Wisconsin Archaeological Reports, vol. 2, Madison, 1989, p. 70, quoted by G. Stacul in *South Asian Archaeology 1989,* p. 268; cf. Jim G. Shaffer, 'The Indus Valley, Baluchistan and Helmand Traditions: Neolithic through Bronze Age', in Robert W. Ehrich, ed., *Chronologies in Old World Archaeology,* vol. I, 1992, p. 459.

places Pirak I-II in *c*. 2000-1300 BC.[37] Terracotta figures of horse riders found in Pirak belong to 1800-1300 BC.

Remains of horse and horse furnishings appear in the burials of the Gandhara grave culture in the Swat valley in 1400 BC and later. The presence of the horse in Pirak, the Gomal valley and the Swat valley can be linked to its spread in north India. In the overlapping layers of the Painted Grey Ware and Harappan cultures at Bhagwanpura in Haryana horse bones appear. These levels are attributed to 1400-1000 BC.[38] The Surkotada horse may have been contemporaneous with the Pirak horse. The horse also appears in late or post-urban Harappan phase at Mohenjodaro, Harappa, Lothal and Ropar. The presence of the horse has been reported neither from recent excavations at Harappa in 1980-93 nor from Dholavira. Similarly the use of the spoked wheel in the mature Harappan phase cannot be established.

The presence of the horse in the late Harappan phase at various places is consistent with its arrival in Pirak and the Swat valley from the eighteenth century BC onwards. The horse becomes important in the non-Harappan/post-Harappan cultures of Pirak, Gandhara and the Painted Grey Ware sites. Horse bones appear in the PGW stratum of Hastinapur around 500 BC, and several places in northern India show terracotta figures of horses and bulls in PGW layers.[39]

[37]Shaffer, op. cit., pp. 458-9.

[38]J.P. Joshi, *Excavation at Bhagwanpura: 1975-76*, ASI, Govt. of India, New Delhi, 1993, pp. 143-7.

[39]A. Ghosh, ed., *An Encyclopaedia of Indian Archaeology*, vol. 1, Munshiram Manoharlal, New Delhi, 1989, pp. 107-8, 338.

Pit-dwelling

Pit-dwelling can also be associated with the Aryan culture, though the Vedic term *gartá*[40] for pit lacks cognates in other Indo-European languages. In the mid-fifth millennium BC the horse-users of the Ukraine lived in semi-subterranean houses in addition to surface houses. With their eastward advance pit-dwelling appeared in the Ural-Volga region in the fourth and third millennia BC, and in the Andronovo culture of Central Asia in the second millennium BC. Burial seems to have developed in imitation of pit-dwelling which may have originated in cold conditions.

Birch

Along with underground houses the use of birch wood seems to be an Aryan feature. In sharp contrast to other arboreal terms *bhūrja* or birch has its cognates in six Indo-European languages.[41] Although this tree is found in a good part of Eurasia including the Ukraine, its earliest remains appear in the Andronovan settlements,[42] where it was used in structures together with pine and cidar.[43] The subterranean dwellings were especially covered with birch.

Cremation

The practice of cremation is supported by the Vedic, Avestan and Homeric texts. It does not seem to be a feature of the mature Harappan culture. The Harappans

[40] *Garta* also means high seat in a chariot; *s.v. garta,* M. Monier-Williams, *A Sanskrit-English Dictionary* (SED).

[41] Mallory, op. cit., p. 275 n. 2.

[42] Ibid., p. 228.

[43] Ibid.

practised earth burial, which underwent a distinct change in their later phase. This is shown by pot burial in Cemetery-H; in some cases the new practice also shows burnt bones deposited in urns. Formerly Cemetery-H was supposed to be confined to Harappa, but now we know of as many as seventy-two sites containing Cemetery-H related materials.[44] Wheeler considers Cemetery-H to be 'alien' and 'more definitely post-Harappan',[45] and it is taken as symbolizing the arrival of a new group of people.

Post-cremation burial appears at several sites in the extension area of the Harappan culture in Gujarat, but it is difficult to date it in this area. Thus the evidence at Surkotada is doubtful. In any case even if we take a liberal view of the chronological position the practice cannot be earlier than 2000 BC, when the post-urban phase begins. Its introduction may be attributed to contact with outside areas where the practice had started much earlier. It is difficult to argue for human cremation on the basis of the burnt bones of birds and animals, as has been done in some cases.[46] Cremation is as old as the fifth millennium BC. Archaeologically its instances occur in Holland, Germany, Eastern Europe, Iraq and Kazakhstan in Central Asia in 5000-4000 BC. Although it is not clear when and where this practice was adopted by horse-users, we know that around 1500 BC they followed it in both Europe and Asia including the Chinese part of eastern Central Asia. In the Indian subcontinent the earliest use of cremation by horse-users occurs in the Swat valley. Wheeler rules out its prevalence

[44]Dani and Masson, op. cit., p. 399.

[45]Wheeler, op. cit., p. 69.

[46]M.K. Dhavalikar, *Cultural Imperialism (Indus Civilization in Western India)*, Books & Books, New Delhi, 1995, p. 200.

both at Harappa and Mohenjodaro,[47] though some late Harappans may have followed it because of outside contacts. At a distance of about 500 km from the Swat area it appears in Tajikistan around 1400 BC.[48]

The fire cult

The fire cult is considered to be a special trait of the Indo-Aryans or Indo-Iranians. The fire altar (*vedi*) is mentioned in the *Ṛg Veda*, and fire worship is very important in the *Avesta*. Some scholars take the fire cult to be Harappan. But the 'fire altars' found in Lothal in Gujarat and Kalibangan in Rajasthan are doubted by the excavators themselves. S.R. Rao suspects Lothal altars to be ovens,[49] and in Kalibangan B.B. Lal calls them altars because no suitable terms are available.[50] In any case it is clear that the fire altars discovered in the Harappan context match neither the textual prescriptions nor the age-old traditional practices. As fire is so indispensable to human existence it may have been worshipped in many regions including the Indus valley, but whether it took the form there of the Vedic altar is extremely doubtful. We may note that some structures not exactly similar to Vedic fire altars, but indicating fire worship, appear in the Ukraine in 4000-3500 BC.[51]

[47]Wheeler, op. cit., p. 68.

[48]Sharma, *Looking for the Aryans*, pp. 52-9.

[49]*Lothal: A Harappan Port Town*, *Memoirs of the Archaeological Survey of India*, no. 78, New Delhi, 1979, pp. 20-1, 96-8, 216-17.

[50]'Some reflections on the structural remains at Kalibanga', in B.B. Lal and S.P. Gupta, eds., *Frontiers of the Indus Civilization*, Books & Books, New Delhi, 1984, p. 57.

[51]Mallory, op. cit., pp. 53, 203-4.

Animal sacrifice

Animal sacrifice was an important ritual of the Aryan culture. But because of its almost universal presence among pastoral tribal people it is difficult to make much of it. The earliest stock raisers did not raise cattle for the sake of milk and dairy products. A segment of the Gond tribe still believes that milk is only meant for the calf. Therefore the early pastoralists were probably great meat eaters. The ritual of animal sacrifice may have evolved because of the need for non-vegetarian food. In the fourth and third millennia BC graves in the Ukraine and south Russia provide many examples of animal sacrifice in funeral ceremonies. Similar cases occur in south Central Asia in the second millennium BC and later. Apparently the ritual prevailed in day-to-day life. What was needed in this world was also provided in the next world.

Horse sacrifice

Animal sacrifice may have prevailed among many tribal peoples, but the horse sacrifice was typical of the Indo-Europeans, particularly of the Vedic people. The French Vedic scholar Louis Renou considers it to be an Indo-European ritual. A good deal of archaeological evidence about the horse sacrifice appears in Eastern, Central, Western and Northern Europe and also in the Caucasus and Central Asia.[52] In the Ukraine and south Russia many cemeteries testify to the sacrifice of more than one horse. The practice seems to have started in the second half of the fifth

[52]Mrityunjay Kumar, 'The Puruṣamedha and Aśvamedha: An Historical Study', Ph.D. Thesis, University of Delhi, 1998, pp. 108-17.

millennium BC. It became widespread in later millennia and continued in Rome and medieval Ireland and Central Asia. Only two hymns are devoted to the horse sacrifice in the tenth *maṇḍala* of the *Ṛg Veda* (162-3), but it is popularised as the *aśvamedha* in later Vedic texts. Animals may have been sacrificed in pre-Vedic times in the subcontinent, but so far archaeological substantiation is wanting. Archaeological evidence regarding the horse sacrifice found in Europe and Central Asia is absent in India. The buffalo sacrifice became an important ritual in the worship of the various forms of Śakti goddess, but because of the rarity of this animal in Eastern Europe and Central Asia the practice did not prevail in those regions.

The cult of soma

The cult of *soma*, called *haoma* in the Avestan language, was confined to the Iranian and Vedic peoples. The identification of the *soma* plant has been debated for long. But now a plant called ephedra whose small twigs appear in vessels used in drinking ritual on the premises of the temple of Togolok-21 in Margiana in south-eastern Turkmenistan[53] is considered to be *soma*. Although this identification[54] is accepted, search for conclusive evidence is continuing.[55]

[53]Asko Parpola, 'The Coming of the Aryans to Iran and India and the Cultural and Ethnic Identity of the Dāsas', *Inernational Journal of Dravidian Linguistics*, XVII, no. 2, pp. 146-7.

[54]Ibid., p. 146.

[55]Harri Nyberg, 'The Problem of the Aryans and the Soma: The botanical evidence', in George Erdosy, ed., op. cit., pp. 382-406.

The svastika (卐)

Sometimes the svastika, an ancient symbol formed by a cross with equal arms, is taken as a mark of Aryanism. It acquired a global importance when the Nazis adopted it as a symbol of unadulterated Aryanism. Unknown to Vedic literature, the term appears in the texts of the early Christian centuries when its manifestation in religious art is considered auspicious. But according to Aurel Stein the symbol first appears in the Shahi Tump Grey Ware culture, which is dated earlier than the Harappan culture and related to the south Iranian.[56] He considers the svastika motif to be unique because no such motif was found in Indian or West Asian cultures.[57] However, Mackay states that the svastika symbol originated in Elam. The svastika-bearing stamps in the Harappan culture and one found in Altyn-depe[58] may belong to 2300-2000 BC.[59] In Shahi Tump the svastika symbol was used on the funerary bowls, and around 1200 BC the grave site was marked with this symbol in the Beshkent cemeteries in south Tajikistan.[60]

Around 800 BC the symbol appears as a decorative piece on Painted Grey Ware used for domestic

[56]H.D. Sankalia, *Prehistory and Protohistory of India and Pakistan*, Deccan College Postgraduate and Research Institute, Pune, 1974, pp. 323-4.

[57]Sankalia, op. cit., pp. 323-4. Though the svastika appears on some Harappan seals, Mackay thinks that it is not peculiar to the Indus valley and adds that it appeared very early in Elam (Ernest Mackay, *Early Indus Civilization*, 2nd enlarged and revd edn, edited by Dorothy Mackay, Luzac, London, 1948 and Indological Book Corporation, Delhi, 1976, pp. 71-2).

[58]V.M. Masson in Dani and Masson, eds., op. cit., p. 242.

[59]Ibid., p. 237.

[60]Dani and Masson, eds., op. cit., p. 394.

purposes.[61] Thus the svastika appears to be not only pre-Vedic but also pre-Harappan in origin. Apparently it spread from Elam and Baluchistan to the Indus valley and Turkmenistan; from Turkmenistan it may have spread to Tajikistan and other parts of Central Asia. How it appeared in Maurya and later art needs to be investigated.

Language and inscriptional evidence

Language is the most important mark of the Aryan culture. Linguists have reconstructed the Proto-Indo-European language, which is considered to have started around the seventh or the sixth millennium BC. The Indo-European language is divided into eastern and western branches, and from *c.* 4500 BC stages are marked in the phonetic development of the eastern branch, i.e. the Proto-Indo-Iranian.[62] But solid evidence for the presence of the Proto-Indo-Iranian or Indo-Aryan language is not earlier than 2300 BC. The first linguistic traces of the Indo-Aryans or Proto-Indians appear on a tablet of the dynasty of Agade in Iraq. It mentions two names reconstructed as Arisena and Somasena, which, according to Harmatta, belong to 2300-2100 BC.[63]

Hittite inscriptions from Anatolia suggest the presence of the speakers of the western branch of the Indo-European language in this area from the nineteenth to the seventeenth centuries BC. The speakers of the eastern branch are represented in the inscriptions of the Kassites and the Mitannis in Mesopotamia from the sixteenth to the

[61]Sankalia, op. cit., p. 403.

[62]J. Harmatta, 'The emergence of the Indo-Iranian languages', in Dani and Masson, eds., *History of Civilizations of Central Asia*, vol. I, pp. 362-6.

[63]Ibid., p. 374.

fourteenth centuries BC. In the absence of any inscriptional evidence for the presence of Indo-Aryans in India it is absurd to argue that the speakers of this language spread from India to Mesopotamia. According to Harmatta the Proto-Indo-Iranian language, which contains loan words from the Caucasian languages and the Fino-Ugraic languages, seems to have developed somewhere between the areas of these two languages.

Some Russian linguists consider the region south of the Caucasus to be the original home of the Indo-European language.[64] This includes eastern Anatolia and northern Mesopotamia. Though eastern Anatolia is not far away from the Black Sea area where the early horse was domesticated, neither the horse nor any other typical traits of the Indo-European culture appears in eastern Anatolia in the sixth-fifth millennia BC.

The finding of the Russian linguists supports an earlier hypothesis of Gordon Childe that Anatolia was the original home of the Aryans. This view has been reinforced by Renfrew. According to him agriculture appeared in eastern Anatolia around the seventh millennium BC, and with its spread the Indo-European language also spread in various directions.[65] The expansion of agriculture could lead to the spread of the language of the agriculturists. But cereals were cultivated in the Early Natufian around 10000 BC, and transition to full scale agriculture took place

[64]T.V. Gamkrelidge and V.V. Ivanov, 'The Migrations of Tribes Speaking the Indo-European Dialects from their Original Home in the Near East to their Historical Habitations in Eurasia', *JIES*, vol. 13, nos. 1-2, 1985, p. 49; *Indo-European and the Indo-Europeans*, pt I: The Text, Mouton de Gruyter, New York, 1995.

[65]C. Renfrew, *Archaeology and Language: The Puzzle of Indo-European Origins*, Penguin, Harmondsworth, 1989.

in the southern Levant or Palestine around 7000 BC.[66] In the sixth and seventh millennia BC agriculture appeared in Iraq, Iran and Pakistani Baluchistan. Hence its origin cannot be confined to eastern Anatolia.Further, agriculture was not an important factor in the life of the earliest speakers of the Indo-European language. Harmatta holds that in the beginning of the sixth millennium BC the eastern and western groups of Indo-European languages had no common agricultural terms.[67] This suggests that the Indo-Europeans adopted the agricultural methods of the area where they went. Again, why did the Aryan language completely disappear from its epicentre? However, Renfrew also considers Central Asia to be an alternative original home of the Aryans. More importantly, though basically an anti-diffusionist, he adopts a diffusionist approach to the Aryan problem.

[66]Romana Unger-Hamilton in *Current Anthropology*, vol. 30, no. 1, Feb. 1989, pp. 102-3.

[67]Harmatta in Dani and Masson, eds., op. cit., p. 359.

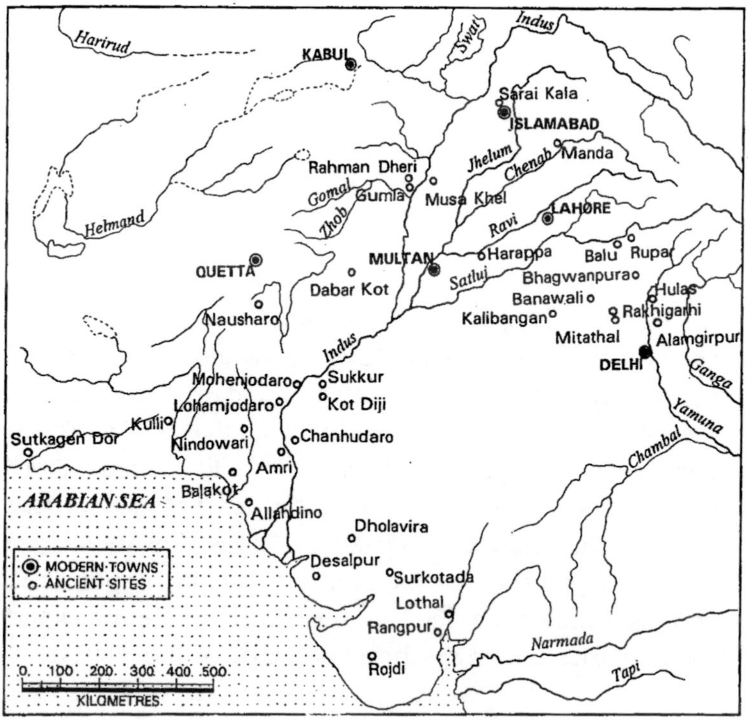

MAP 1: DISTRIBUTION OF INDUS CIVILIZATION.

CHAPTER 2

Was the Harappan Culture Ṛg Vedic and Sarasvati-based?

How far was the Harappan culture Sarasvati-based?

Some archaeologists regard India as the original home of the Aryans which they place in the Sarasvati basin. According to S.P. Gupta 'the Indus-Sarasvati Civilization represents one very important aspect of the developed Vedic Civilization'. He adds that the Harappan culture was the gift of both the rivers and 'perhaps more of the latter' (Sarasvati). He thinks in terms of Indus *versus* Sarasvati and India *versus* Pakistan. In his view more than 700 Harappan sites on the Sarasvati and its tributaries in contrast to not even 100 Harappan sites on the Indus and its tributaries underline the importance of the Sarasvati.[1]

But we cannot gloss over the other aspects of the comparison between the Indus and the Sarasvati. To begin with, the Sarasvati is identified with the Ghaggar or the Hakra. The river is called Ghaggar in Punjab, Haryana and Rajasthan, and Hakra beyond the Indian border in Pakistan. It must be clearly understood that the Hakra-

[1]S.P. Gupta in S.P. Gupta, ed., *The 'Lost' Sarasvati and the Indus Civilization*, Kusumanjali Publishers, Jodhpur, 1995, pp. 181-4.

Ghaggar is a tributary of the Indus.[2] Further, none of the major Harappan sites including Harappa, Mohenjodaro and Dholavira is located on the Hakra or Ghaggar; only Kalibangan is close to the Ghaggar. Banawali in Hisar district is not as important as Kalibangan, and Kunal in the same district cannot be taken as a Harappan site because of its own distinct characteristics. No Harappan settlements appear in Ambala and Sirsa districts where the Ghaggar is important. This is the finding of R.C. Thakran who has surveyed the Harappan sites in Haryana. According to him the dry bed of the Ghaggar has 55 pre-Harappan or early Harappan, 117 mature Harappan and 581 late Harappan sites[3]. A similar survey made in the Hakra area in the Cholistan desert (Bahawalpur) in Pakistan by M.R. Mughal shows 40 early Harappan, 174 mature Harappan and 50 late Harappan sites.[4] Thakran's survey shows that a good many people from decaying towns in the south-west migrated towards the north-east and settled in the Ghaggar area in the late Harappan phase. We notice a sharp contrast between the upper and lower basin of the dried up Sarasvati. While settlements dramatically fall in number in Cholistan in the Hakra area in the post-urban period,[5] 581 post-urban settlements appear in the Ghaggar area. But far

[2]M. Rafique Mughal, in Gregory L. Possehl, ed., *Ancient Cities of the Indus*, Vikas Publishing House, New Delhi, 1979, p. 91.

[3]Information from R.C. Thakran.

[4]M. Rafique Mughal, 'Recent Archaeological Research in the Cholistan Desert', in Gregory L. Possehl, ed., *Harappan Civilization: A Contemporary Perspective*, Oxford and IBH, New Delhi, 1982, pp. 116-19.

[5]Bridget Allchin and Raymond Allchin, *Origins of a Civilization, The Prehistory and Early Archaeology of South Asia*, Viking, New Delhi, 1997, p. 213.

more urban sites appear on the Pakistani Sarasvati than on the Indian Sarasvati.

However, we need adequate data to draw any firm conclusion from such surveys. Though Mughal gives the size and culture content of some sites, I have not been able to get such data from Thakran; S.P. Gupta also does not help us. We have to know the size of each site as well as the extent and nature of its Harappan culture. For example, according to Mughal 50 late Harappan sites in Bahawalpur or Cholistan show Cemetery-H-related materials,[6] but, as shown later, these contents symbolize the coming of a new people because of a new type of pottery and burnt bones found in the graves. In this sense these sites in the dry bed of the Hakra may contain Aryan elements also.

Until 1981 nearly 750 PGW culture sites were found in Punjab, Haryana, western UP and Rajasthan, and about 450 NBPW culture sites in the mid-Ganga plains.[7] But most of these sites including the Harappan are labelled on the basis of potsherds found in them. Because of this, key sites such as Harappa and Mohenjodaro may be equal to hundreds of Harappan sites in the Ghaggar-Hakra zone. Therefore on the basis of the present data the Sarasvati sites cannot surpass the Sindhu sites.

The Hakra or the Ghaggar basin is only one of the several areas which show the earliest elements of the Harappan culture. Kot Diji and 72 Kot Diji Phase sites located in the central Indus valley region are far more important. 'The KD Phase clearly was critical in the development of the Harappan Phase, or Indus Valley

[6]Mughal in S.P. Gupta, ed., op. cit., p. 119.

[7]R.S. Sharma, *Material Culture and Social Formations in Ancient India*, Macmillan, Delhi, 1997, Appendix II.

Civilization.'[8] Several sites in Baluchistan also reveal some elements of the Harappan culture. Hence the Sarasvati can neither be called a major contributor to the Harappan culture nor equated with the Indus in this respect. If in future the Sarasvati sites reveal Harappan cultural contents that excel those of the well-known Harappan sites outside the Hakra and the Ghaggar zone the Sarasvati will certainly get far more credit. But even this will not justify the renaming of the Indus civilization, for after all the Sarasvati is a tributary of the Indus.

The fundamentalists want to establish the superiority of the Sarasvati over the Indus because of communal considerations. In the Harappan context they think that after partition the Indus belongs to the Muslims and only the Sarasvati remains with the Hindus.[9] The Sarasvati receives much attention in the *Ṛg Veda* and several *sūktas* are devoted to it; so they want to use it for their purpose. But it seems that there are several Sarasvatis, and the earliest Sarasvati cannot be identified with the Hakra and the Ghaggar. In the *Ṛg Veda* the Sarasvati is called the best of the rivers (*nadītama*). It seems to have been a great river with perennial water. The Hakra and the Ghaggar cannot match it. The earliest Sarasvati is considered identical with the Helmand in Afghanistan which is called Harakhwati in the *Avesta*. But the archaeology of the Helmand valley in the second millennium BC needs adequate attention. Its two large cities Shahr-i-Sokhta and Mundigak show decay in this period. In place of wheel-turned pottery

[8]Jim G. Shaffer and B.K. Thapar in A.H. Dani and V.M. Masson, eds., *History of Civilizations of Central Asia*, vol. I, UNESCO Publishing, Paris, 1992, pp. 272-3.

[9]S.P. Gupta in S.P. Gupta, ed., op. cit., pp. 181-3.

Mundigak V shows hand-turned pottery.[10] The users of this pottery may have come from outside, but we need more information about them. In any case the linguistic and time-place proximity of the *Avesta* to the *Ṛg Veda* leaves no doubt that the early Vedic Sarasvati is the same as the Harakhwati or the Helmand. As the Vedic people expanded they took the name Sarasvati to Punjab, Haryana and Rajasthan, and also to Garhwal, Pryaga and Rajgir. A river of this name also appears in both West Bengal and Gujarat. Similarly the Ṛg Vedic Sarayu, identical with the Avestan Harirud in Afghanistan, became the Ramayanic Sarayu in Ayodhya. Sarayu occurs in the fourth, fifth and tenth *maṇḍalas* of the *Ṛg Veda*, and two Arya chiefs had settled on its bank.[11] As the Aryan settlers moved eastward from the bank of the Harirud they carried the river name along with them. This also happened with those who had settled on the bank of the Ṛg Vedic Gomati or the present Gomal in Baluchistan. Now a river in Lucknow bears this name. The river Godavari near its source is called Gomati, which is also the name of a river in Gujarat on which Dwaraka is situated. A branch of the Chambal in Malwa is also known as Gomati.[12] According to the *Rāmāyaṇa*, Rājagṛha or Girivraja was the best city in the land of the Kekayas in western Panjab.[13] Obviously this name was transferred later to Magadha.

[10] V.M. Masson, 'The decline of the Bronze Age Civilization and movements of the tribes', in Dani and Masson, eds. op. cit., pp. 352, 354.

[11] *The Hymns of the Ṛgveda*, tr., Ralph T.H. Griffith, Motilal Banarsidass, Delhi, rpt, 1986, IV. 30.18.

[12] Nando Lal Dey, *The Geographical Dictionary of Ancient and Medieval India*, Oriental Books Reprint Corporation, New Delhi, 1971, p. 70.

[13] H.C. Raichaudhury, *Political History of Ancient India*, University of Calcutta, 1972, p. 57.

Was the Harappan culture Ṛg Vedic?

Some archaeologists think that the Harappa culture was created by the Ṛg Vedic people. In 1978 this was covincingly refuted by B.B. Lal[14] in terms of the time-frame, geography and the cultural contents of the *Ṛg Veda* and Harappa. But in 1997 he becomes a convert to the view he had controverted. He does not accept the chronological gap between Harappa and 'the Vedic texts', points to the presence of the horse in the Harappa culture, and dismisses the theory of the '"glaring disparity" between the cultures represented by the Harappan remains and the Vedic texts'.[15]

The Vedic texts, according to the general consensus of the Vedic scholars, belong to *c*. 1500-500 BC. The *Ṛg Veda* may be placed in the late or post-urban phase of the Harappa period; it cannot be linked to the mature Harappan phase. Lal produces the fundamentalist argument that the *Aitareya Brāhmaṇa* refers to the shifting of the vernal equinox from Mṛgaśiras to Rohiṇi, which occurred around 3500 BC, and thus he places the *Ṛg Veda* in the fourth millennium BC.[16] But modern astronomers who have studied the original texts state that 'the equinoxes are not explicitly mentioned in the Brāhmaṇas'.[17] It should be noted that the *nakṣatras* do not move but the point of the equinox moves. However, the movement of the point of

[14]B.B. Lal, 'The Indo-Aryan Hypothesis *vis-a-vis* Indian Archaeology', *Journal of Central Asia*, vol. 1, no. 1, July 1978, pp. 21-41.

[15]B.B. Lal, *The Earliest Civilization of South Asia*, Aryan Books International, New Delhi, 1997, pp. 281-7.

[16]Ibid., p. 286.

[17]S.N. Sen in D.M. Bose, S.N. Sen and B.V. Subbrayappa, eds., *A Concise History of Science in India*, National Science Academy, New Delhi, 1971, p. 77.

the equinox or *viṣuvat* when day and night are of the same duration is neither mentioned in the Vedas and the Brāhmaṇas nor in the Vedāṅga Jyotiṣa.[18] Hence there is no ground for placing the *Ṛg Veda* in the fourth millennium BC. More importantly, in view of its geography and close similarity with the *Zend Avesta* the *Ṛg Veda* cannot be dated in isolation. The mention of the exact names of the Vedic deities in the Mitanni inscription of the fourteenth century BC clearly shows that the *Ṛg Veda* cannot be much earlier than the fifteenth century BC. A good many archaeological traces of the horse from the Ṛg Vedic area belong to *c.* 1500 BC.

Pleading for the Vedic identity of the Harappan culture, Lal states: 'Just as there were cities, towns and villages in the Harappan ensemble (as there are even today in any society) there were both rural and urban settlements in the Vedic times.' But linguists and archaeologists who have worked on this subject reject this view. 'Linguistically, the Indo-Iranians reveal no cities, fortifications, palaces, temples, writing, irrigation, specialized crafts or trade.'[19] This finding applies to both Proto-Indians and Proto-Iranians. However, Lal quotes the *Ṛg Veda* verse X. 101.8 with Griffith's translation in which the gods are asked 'to make iron forts, secure from all assailants'.[20] Though he rightly questions the meaning of *āyasi pur* as

[18]M.N. Saha and N.C. Lahiri, *History of the Calender*, Council of Scientific and Industrial Research, New Delhi, 1955, rpt, 1992, Appendix 5-D; cf. Sankara Balakrishna Dikshit, *Bharatiya Jyotisa*, Hindi Samiti, Suchana Vibhag, Uttar Pradesh, Lucknow, 2nd edn, 1963.

[19]Y.Y. Kuzmina and K.F. Smirnov, 'The Origin of the Indo-Iranians in the Light of Recent Archaeological Data', *Journal of Central Asia*, vol. 1, no. 1, 1978, p. 68.

[20]Lal, 1997, op. cit., pp. 284-5.

iron fort, he asserts that *pur* means a fortified town.[21] The Vedic people had their *purs*, for there is the story that to fight the Asuras effectively the Devas set up the counter-*purs* and also counter-kingship. But those who have adequately examined references to *pur* in the Vedic texts, particularly in the *Ṛg Veda*, do not consider it a fortified town. Wilhelm Rau, a Vedicist, and George Erdosy, an archaeologist, do not identify the Vedic settlements with the Harappan.[22] According to Rau, 'Not a word is said in our texts of the characteristic features of the Indus cities, of brick walls, brick houses, brick-paved streets laid out on an orthogonal pattern, of granaries or public baths.' He holds that towns are mentioned at the very end of the Vedic period.[23] Erdosy elaborates the idea of Macdonell and Keith,[24] and questions the very existence of *pur* in the sense of fort on contextual grounds. Thus he considers 're-newed insistence on equating the Ṛgvedic and Harappan civilizations' to be 'eccentric assertions'.[25] In our opinion the myths and metaphors relating to the *pur* suggest that it was either a dwelling unit or a cluster of such units as appeared in the post-urban Harappan phase. Particularly the early Vedic stone *purs* may represent the recently discovered rock shelters in which pastoralists lived in the hilly tracts of the North-West Frontier.

[21]Ibid.

[22]Wilhelm Rau, *The Meaning of pur in Vedic Literature*, Wilhelm Fink Verlag, Munchen, 1976; George Erdosy, 'The meaning of Ṛgvedic *pur*: Notes on the Vedic landscape', in Jonathan Mark Kenoyer, ed., *From Sumer to Meluha: Contributions to the Archaeology of South and East Asia in Memory of George F. Dales Jr.*, Wisconsin Archaeological Reports, vol. 3, Madison, 1994, pp. 223-34.

[23]Rau, 1976, op. cit., p. 52.

[24]*Vedic Index of Names and Subjects*, 1912, Motilal Banarsidass, Delhi, vol. I, rpt, 1967, pp. 538-9.

[25]Erdosy, 1994, op. cit., pp. 224, 232.

Lal finds 'ample evidence . . . of sea-trade', and speaks of 'tremendous wealth' obtained from it. In support he quotes a verse from the ninth Book of the *Ṛg Veda* together with its translation by Griffith.[26] The verse reads: '*rāyaḥ samudrānscaturoasmabhyam soma viśvataḥ, ā pavasva sahasriṇaḥ*'.[27] The translation reads: 'From every side, O Soma, for our profit, pour thou forth four seas filled full of riches thousandfold.' We may add that the ninth Book in which this verse occurs is devoted exclusively to Sōma, and added to the main text later. Further, Griffith's translation of *asmabhyam* as *for our profit* creates an impression of profit arising out of trade; such a confusion is not created by Geldner.[28] We should also note that the four seas are called imaginary by Griffith.[29]

In this context the commentary of Sāyaṇa makes more sense. According to Sāyaṇa the sacrificer prays to Soma for the possession of the whole world bounded by the four seas.[30] In any case there is no reference whatsoever to 'tremendous' wealth acquired from 'sea-trade.' This does not mean that the early Vedic people were unfamiliar with the seas. V.I. Sarianidi[31] and R.N. Nandi[32] suggest that people migrated to the Indus valley along the Persian Gulf and the Makran coast. Nandi has looked into

[26]Lal, 1997, op. cit., p. 285.

[27]IX. 33.6.

[28]*Harvard Oriental Series*, vol. 35, 1951, p. 30.

[29]*The Hymns of the Ṛgveda*, Motilal Banarsidass, Delhi, rpt, 1986, p. 483.

[30]*catuḥsamudramudritabhūmaṇḍalasvāmitvam eva aśāste yajamānaḥ*. Comm. on *ṚV*, IX. 33.6 in *Ṛg-Veda-Saṃhitā*, vol. III, ed., F. Max Müller, Oxford University Press, London, 1892.

[31]*Journal of Central Asia*, vol. 1, no. 1, 1978, p. 77.

[32]*Indian Historical Review*, vol. XXI, nos. 1 and 2, 1994-5, pp. 9-36.

most references to the sea in the *Ṛg Veda*. On the basis of those from Books I and X he speaks of 'peddling of goods' and 'petty trading' in the context of land trade,[33] but we cannot infer sea trade from these references.

The early Vedic people were primarily pastoral though their agriculture was not negligible. Though rich in vocabulary, apart from buying and selling, the *Ṛg Veda* has no term for commerce as a specific activity.[34] Its early portions have no term for leasing or hiring, for lending or borrowing. Though the term *ṛṇa* appears in the early portions, it indicates a mutual obligation to pay. The *Ṛg Veda* does not know of slaves, wage-earners or hired labourers engaged in production.[35] And yet all these features can be expected if its culture were urban. Fired bricks are a striking feature of the Harappans, and no Bronze Age civilization can boast of them on such a large scale. But this important construction material is unknown to the *Rg Veda*. In Wheeler's view there is no granary in the pre-classical world comparable in specialization of design and in monumental dignity to the examples from the two Indus cities.[36] But because of the absence of urbanism the Vedic people did not need granary, and consequently the *Ṛg Veda* has no term for it.

Since the Harappan script has not been decoded we may leave it out for the present. But the animals portrayed on the inscribed objects certainly deserve attention. According to the analysis of I. Mahadevan, as

[33]Ibid., pp. 34-5.

[34]R.S. Sharma, *Material Culture and Social Formations in Ancient India*, pp. 30-1

[35]Ibid.

[36]R.E.M. Wheeler, *The Indus Civilization*, 3rd edn, Cambridge University Press, Bentley House, London, 1968, p. 36.

many as 1164 objects depict the unicorn as a field animal.[37] But in the Harappan context it is taken to be a fabulous animal resembling perhaps an ox. Nevertheless in our view the unicorn should be considered a fabulous rhinoceros because of its one horn. The Harappan unicorn shows one long horn and a short hump close to it which is exactly the case with the rhinoceros. However, in addition to what is called the unicorn, the rhinoceros is clearly portrayed on about 40 inscribed objects.[38] Thus the one-horned animal is associated with as many as 1204 inscribed objects including seals. Wheeler notes that this animal is most frequently represented on the Harappan seals.[39] In the seals and sealings of Lothal the unicorns form the overwhelming majority of the animal symbols. But this most favourite animal of the Harappans is not known to the *Ṛg Veda.* The term *gaṇḍa* or *khadga* is used for the rhinoceros in Sanskrit, and the term *ekaśṛṅga* for both the unicorn and the rhinoceros, but none of these terms occur in the *Ṛg Veda.* Significantly enough, with *gaṇḍa* and *khaḍga* are of non-Aryan origin.

On the other hand, the horse, the hallmark of the early Vedic culture, is neither a trait of the early nor of the mature Harappan culture. Lal refers to horse remains in the Harappan sites of Mohenjodaro, Lothal, Surkotada and Kalibangan,[40] and S.P. Gupta adds Harappa, Malvan and Rana Ghundai to this list,[41] but what about the date, number and authenticity of these traces? Rao, an older champion of the Aryan Harappa, places the skeletal remains

[37]Quoted in B.V. Subbarayappa, *Indus Script*, New Era Publications, Chennai, 1996, Table 15.

[38]Ibid.

[39]Wheeler, op. cit., p. 102.

[40]Lal, 1997, op. cit., p. 285.

[41]S.P. Gupta, op. cit.

of the horse in Lothal and Mohenjodaro in their late levels.[42] He adds that the presence of the animal in Mohenjodaro, Harappa, Lothal and Ropar is restricted to the later phase of the Harappan culture.[43] Malvan is not even a Harappan site, and its Period I in which horse bones appear first is 'essentially a post-Harappan, Chalcolithic occupation'.[44] The horse reported from Rana Ghundai in Baluchistan is attributed to the third millennium BC, but has been found to be a half ass or onager on examination.[45] More importantly, considering a good many excavations in the large Harappan area horse traces are few. That is why Lal 'would like to have more and more examples'.[46] According to him, the evidence from Pakistan is 'meagre' though 'positive'. He admits that Harappa's earlier excavator Vats, and its current excavators Meadow and Kenoyer, have not reported any horse bones from the site. He, however, refers to the remains of the horse in an earlier collection from the site. But even if we accept it, it does not mean much. The existing evidence shows that the life of the Harappans was not horse-centred, as was the case with the early Vedic people, particularly their chiefs. Further, the *Ṛg Veda* is full of war.[47] The early Vedic assemblies including the *gaṇa, sabhā, samiti, vidatha* and *parisad* performed military functions

[42]Rao, *Lothal and the Indus Civilization*, Asia Publishing House, Bombay, 1973, p. 89.

[43]S.R. Rao, *Lothal: A Harappan Port Town*, Memoirs of the Archaeological Survey of India, no. 78, New Delhi, 1979, p. 219.

[44]F.R. Allchin and Jagat Pati Joshi, *Excavations at Malvan*, Archaeological Survey of India, New Delhi, 1995, pp. 5, 15.

[45]Bridget and Raymond Allchin, *The Birth of Indian Civilization*, Penguin, Harmondsworth, 1968, p. 103.

[46]Lal, 1997, op. cit., p. 286.

[47]Sharma, *Material Culture and Social Formations in Ancient India*, Chap. 3.

also.[48] The importance of warfare in the life of the Vedic people is brought out in a well-researched monograph by Sarva Daman Singh.[49] He points out that although the Harappans were fully familiar with the wheeled vehicle there is 'no proof of the battle-chariot before the advent of the Aryans'.[50] Similarly the spoked wheel known to the *Ṛg Veda* was not in use in the mature Harappan phase. The absence of the war chariot and the spoked wheel is consistent with the military weakness of the Harappans, which has been underlined by several archaeologists.[51] According to Wheeler, the military element does not loom large amongst the extant Harappan remains.[52]

We may not look for Vedic bows and quivers in the Harappan remains, but even other weapons are very poorly represented. On the other hand the Indo-Aryan archaeological complex of *c.* 1900-1700 BC in south Turkmenistan and north Afghanistan shows 'abundance of weapons'. This 'suggests that the ruling elite . . . was actively engaged in warfare'.[53] Certain tools and implements could be common to all Neolithic and Bronze Age societies, but that does not establish specific similarity. However, unlike the Harappan culture, bronze did not enjoy a crucial place in the Aryan culture. In the mounted nomadic

[48]Sharma, *Aspects of Political Ideas and Institutions in Ancient India*, Motilal Banarsidass, Delhi, 1996, Chaps. 7-10.

[49]Singh, *Ancient Indian Warfare with Special Reference to the Vedic Period*, E.J. Brill, Leiden, 1965.

[50]Ibid., p. 168.

[51]B.B. Lal in B.B. Lal and S.P. Gupta, eds., *Frontiers of the Indus Civilization*, Books & Books, New Delhi, 1984, p. 55; cf. K.M. Srivastava, ibid., p. 437.

[52]Wheeler, op. cit., p. 73.

[53]Asko Parpola in Erdosy, ed., *The Indo-Aryans of Ancient South Asia*, 1st Indian edn, Munshiram Manoharlal, New Delhi, 1997, pp. 361, 374.

conditions of north Central Asia bronze did not play the same role as it did in the sedentary conditions of Harappa, Mesopotamia and Crete or even in the proto-urban cultures of south Central Asia. Because of this, terms for tin or bronze are absent in the *Ṛg Veda*. The Aryans were basically pastoralists who adopted the skills and crafts of sedentary people on their arrival in India. This explains the presence in the *Ṛg Veda* of agricultural terms which do not occur in other ancient Indo-European languages.[54] Of the three terms, *vṛka, sīra* and *lāṅgala*, each used for the plough in the *Ṛg Veda*, only the first has parallels in Indo-European languages. The term *phāla* which means ploughshare in the *Ṛg Veda* does not have any Indo-European cognate. *Sītā* is represented in this text as the presiding deity over agriculture, but this term also lacks Indo-European cognates.[55] The *Śatapatha Brāhmaṇa*, a later Vedic text of about the seventh century BC, suggests that the pre-Aryans of India were mostly engaged in agriculture. According to it (I.6.1.4) even the foremost of the Asuras ploughed the fields and sowed the seeds, and those behind them carried on reaping and threshing. The gods considered these agricultural activities damaging to their prospects of victory in war. Hence they tried to upset the agricultural activities of the Asuras. It seems that ultimately they took to these activities in their own interest as they did when they adopted the Asura kingship and *pur*.

Last, the Ṛg Vedic society is male-dominated, while Harappa shows the dominance of the mother cult in religion.

[54]Sharma, *Material Culture and Social Formations in Ancient India*, pp. 25-6.

[55]*s.v. vṛka, sīra, lāṅgala, sītā* and *phāla*, Monier-Williams, *SED*; Gy. Wojtilla, 'The Sanskrit Terminology of the Plough', *Acta Orientalia Academiae Scientiarum Hung Tomus*, XLII, nos. 2-3, 1988, pp. 325-38.

In my opinion the archaeological counterpart of the *Ṛg Veda* in the subcontinent appears in the post-Harappan sites of the North-West Frontier and Baluchistan. These sites show the horse, cremation, pit-dwellings and also some pottery paintings known in Iran.

It is argued by some that the Aryans went from India to Western Asia. But where is the evidence for the presence of the Aryans in India around 2300 BC when the earliest specimens of their language appear in Mesopotamia? If the Aryans used the Harappan script why did they not take it to Western Asia? When the Buddhists went to Central Asia they carried the Brāhmī script, and under the Kuṣāṇas Prakrit inscriptions appear in Brāhmī and Kharoṣṭhī in Bactria. Buddhist manuscripts appear in Turfan and Khotan. Since the Aryans did not have writing, examples of their language appear in cuneiform script and the Hittite hieroglyphs. The Proto-Elamite script became extinct in about 2800 BC,[56] and the Harappan in about 1900 BC. So the Aryans could not use any of these. Though the Proto-Indo-Aryans and the Proto-Indo-Iranians lived in north and south Central Asia from *c.* 2500 BC onwards because of the absence of writing in those regions even in the second millennium BC we have no specimen of their written language. It is a misfortune for the champions of the Indian origin of the Aryans that there is no inscriptional evidence of Aryan presence in India. But in discussing this problem we cannot ignore such evidence from Western Asia. We cannot study the *Ṛg Veda* in complete isolation from the general cultural development of the ancient world. All told, the attempt to impose a Vedic identity on the Harappan culture resembles similar attempts to exploit

[56]M. Tosi et al., in Dani and Masson, eds., op. cit., p. 199.

archaeology for political purposes in Spain, Portugal, Germany, Russia, China, Japan and several other countries.[57]

The Indus culture and the Ganga culture

While attempts are made to identify the Vedic culture with the Harappan, the importance of the Vedic culture and its archaeological counterparts is ignored by emphasizing the impact of the Harappan tradition on the Ganga culture. Some archaeologists notice Harappan influence in the mid-Ganga chalcolithic and later cultures.[58] Stray elements of the Harappan culture such as beads may have reached the Ganga plains, but they did not form its distinctive feature. Neither the basic traits of the PGW/later Vedic culture in the upper Ganga plains nor those of the NBPW/early Pali texts culture in the mid-Ganga plains had Harappan ancestry. General modes of subsistence such as agriculture, cattle keeping and elementary crafts may share common features in a good part of the subcontinent in the first millennium BC. But what about such diagnostic Harappan traits as town life, fired bricks and script in the PGW phase? Even when the script appeared in the mid-NBPW phase it was entirely different from the Harappan.

[57]Sharma, Review of L. Kohl and Clare Fawcett, eds., *Nationalism, Politics and the Practice of Archaeology*, Cambridge University Press, Bentley House, London, 1995, *Newsletter of Archaeology, Anthropology, History, South Asia Network*, Issue 5/Summer 1997, pp. 17-18; Romila Thapar, 'The Theory of Aryan Race and India: History and Politics', *Transactions of the International Conference of Eastern Studies*, no. XL, 1995, pp. 41-65.

[58]Jonathan Mark Kenoyer, 'Interaction systems, specialised crafts and culture change: The Indus Valley Tradition and the Indo-Gangetic Tradition in South Asia', in George Erdosy, ed., op. cit., pp. 213-57.

The Harappans wrote from right to left while Brāhmī was written from left to right. The effective use of iron inaugurated a new socio-economic structure in the mid-Ganga plains in the fifth century BC. But iron was not derived from the Indus culture, and so is the case with coinage which also played a vital role in the new structure.

The PGW made a complete break with the Harappan tradition of pottery. The Harappans practised open kiln firing while the PGW potters practised closed kiln firing. The latter manufactured dishes and bowls in contrast to the dish-on-stand, goblets, storage-jars, etc., of the Harappans. Even as older local connections may be expected, PGW pottery cannot be traced back to any chalcolithic pottery. On the basis of Noh and Atranjikhera Misra traces nearly 50 per cent of the PGW types to the Black-and-Red Ware. But he also notes the stratigraphical gap between the two wares at both sites.[59] How do we explain the transformation of the ordinary early ware into the later de luxe PGW? Is it due to external influence?

Similarly, the NBPW held nothing in common with the Harappan ceramic tradition. To date weights and measures used in NBPW times are not known to us with certainty. Accidental similarites between Harappan weights and weights of coins in the Kauṭilyan *Arthaśāstra* are rightly attributed to the availability of the same type of seeds in different parts of the country.[60] According to Wheeler, the Harappan foot seems to vary between 13.0 and 13.2 inches while the Harappan cubit ranges from 20.3 to 20.6 inches.[61] Such measures are not known in the NBPW

[59]V.D. Misra, 'Origin and Antiquity of the Painted Grey Ware', *University of Allahabad Studies*, vol. 2 (n.s.), no. 1, Jan. 1970, pp. 11-24.

[60]Kenoyer, op. cit., p. 233.

[61]Wheeler, *The Indus Civilization*, 1968, p. 84.

phase. Pre-industrial weights and measures varied from area to area. Early medieval inscriptions show that land measures differ from region to region according to the length of the hand of the local ruler.

If the Aryans came from outside, it is said, why did not they bring tin for making bronze?[62] We may refer to the famous bronze dagger of the twelfth century BC from Fort Munro in the Sulaiman range west of the Indus, which came from the north-west or the direction of the 'Aryan invasions' [63] A shaft-hole bronze axe found at Chanhudaro in a late Harappan layer[64] may have come from the same direction. Similar is the case of a fine copper axe-adze which has its analogues at three places in north Iran and at two places in north Caucasia.[65] The Allchins mention other stray finds of copper and bronze objects but add that several finds are not datable in themselves.[66] Despite these examples, bronze did not play a pivotal role in the life of the Aryans who were basically a pastoral people. It is because of this that terms for tin and bronze do not occur in the *Ṛg Veda*. When bronze appeared in the Ganga plains tin did not come from Afghanistan but most probably from the south Bihar plateau and its rich deposits in Bastar in Madhya Pradesh. Yet, how the people of the Ganga plains learnt to alloy tin with copper and manufacture bronze needs to be investigated. In kin-based societies technology may have been diffused through migrations,[67] but the situation may have been different in class- and caste-based

[62]Kenoyer, op. cit., p. 230.

[63]Wheeler, op. cit., p. 133.

[64]Ibid., p. 75.

[65]Ibid.

[66]Bridget Allchin and Raymond Allchin, *The Birth of Indian Civilization*, Penguin, Harmondsworth, 1968, pp. 144-53.

[67]Cf. Kenoyer, op. cit., pp. 216-17.

societies. The mature Harappan culture could not be basically kin-based. However, artisans looking for subsistence and rehabilitation may have spread technology after the desertions of the Harappan settlements around 2000 BC, the chalcolithic settlements in central and western India around 1000 BC, and the urban settlements in a major part of the country in AD 300-600. Such desertions explode the myth of cultural continuity in some areas, and open the possibility for diffusion in other areas.[68]

The disappearance of the Harappan writing is attributed either to the breakdown of long-distance trade[69] or to the dominance of the Vedic ritual-ridden priests.[70] The first explanation is too simplistic. Long-range trade shrank substantially for nearly three centuries after *c.* AD 600 in India,[71] but writing continued as usual. How the Vedic priests extinguished the Indus writing is a mystery; some archaeologists argue that Harappan society was dominated by the priests. The only possible explanation is the influx of numerous pre-literate pastoralists who did not need writing. However, their arrival eventually led to the spread of horse, spoked wheel, cremation, fire cult and, above all, the Indo-Aryan language in the mid-Ganga plains. Perhaps the Proto-Dravidian and Austric dialects were spoken in pre-NBPW pockets as is suggested by their random survivals in the mid-Ganga plains. In several ancient societies the victorious were culturally conquered

[68]Sharma, *The State and Varna Formation in the Mid-Ganga Plains: An Ethnoarchaeological View*, Manohar, New Delhi, 1996, p. 33; *Urban Decay in India (c. 300-c.1000)*, Munshiram Manoharlal, New Delhi, 1987, Chap. 8.

[69]Kenoyer, op. cit., p. 223.

[70]Ibid., p. 234.

[71]Sharma, 1987, op. cit., Chap. 8.

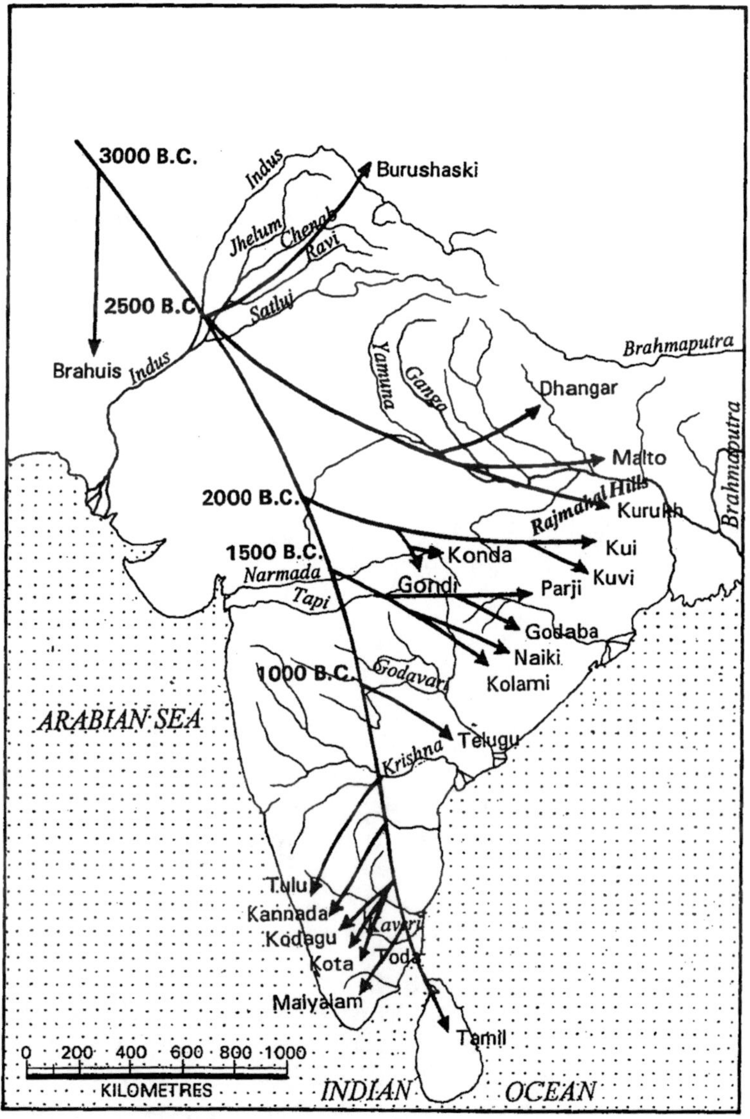

MAP 2: ROUTES OF THE HISTORICAL SETTLEMENTS OF DRAVIDIANS IN THE SUBCONTINENT.

by the vanquished, but the Indo-Aryan immigrants seem to have been numerous and strong enough to continue and disseminate much of their culture. Wheeler's theory of the Aryan destruction of the Indus culture cannot be proved archaeologically, but his view[72] that the Indus civilization utterly failed to transmit itself beyond its primary homeland will hold good until adequate data to the contrary are available.

[72]Wheeler, op. cit., p. 137.

CHAPTER 3

Linguistic and Archaeological Evidence for the Aryan Arrival

Linguistic difference

The *Ṛg Veda* suggests that the people whom the Aryans encountered spoke a language different from their own. The term *mṛdhravāc* is applied to the Dasyus and Paṇis who were the great enemies of the Aryans. It is also applied to other opponents. Though this term is translated as 'insulting' or 'hostile' speech, in his Sanskrit texts Muir renders it as 'stammering or unintelligible' speech. Hillebrandt translates the term as 'speaking an enemy's speech'. Even when it is applied to the Purus in the *Ṛg Veda* he takes it in the sense of a different dialect, and suggests that the Purus were dialectically different from the Bharatas.[1] Sāyaṇa takes *mṛdhravāc* in the sense of *bādhavāc*, which may mean hostile speech, but in view of the ethnicity of the Dasyus[2] this term may convey the sense of unintelligible speech.

[1]A.A. Macdonell and A.B. Keith, *Vedic Index of Names and Subjects*, vol. I, Motilal Banarsidass, Delhi, 3rd rpt, 1967, pp. 347-9 with fns. 11 and 12 on p. 348.

[2]R.S. Sharma, *Śūdras in Ancient India*, 3rd edn, Motilal Banarsidass, Delhi, 1990, pp. 13-16, 25-6.

Use of Dravidian in the north

Since the Harappan script has not been deciphered we have to think of other types of data regarding the languages of the Harappan and non-Vedic peoples. We still find Brahui-speaking people in Baluchistan. In Harappan times Brahui seems to have belonged to a family of northern Dravidian linked with the Elamite language and prevalent in south Iran, Afghanistan and Baluchistan.[3] Most Brahuis are bilingual. The 1961 Census of Pakistan records Brahui as the mother tongue of nearly 400,000 persons. They are confined not only to Baluchistan but are also found in Sind. Brahui is also spoken in parts of Afghanistan, Iran and Turkmenistan. Around 1980 the total number of Brahui speakers was estimated at 600,000.[4]

Recent linguistic researches show that the Dravidian-speaking people were present in the Indus valley, in both the Harappan and post-Harappan periods.[5] At present, besides the prevalence of the two Dravidian dialects in the Brahui area of Baluchistan,[6] we find remnants of Dravidian language in North-West Frontier region and in Kashmir. We encounter a dialect called Burushaski which is spoken in Pakistan-occupied Kashmir and adjoining regions. Whether it is Dardic or Dravidian is a matter of dispute, but this speech contains a good many terms

[3]Sharma, *Looking for the Aryans*, pp. 67-70.

[4]M.S. Andronov, *Dravidian Languages,* 'Nauka' Publishing House, Moscow, 1970, p. 23; *The Brahui Language*, 'Nauka' Publishing House, Moscow, 1980, p. 15.

[5]Franklin C. Southworth, 'Reconstructing Social Context from Language; Indo-Aryan and Dravidian Prehistory', in George Erdosy, ed., op. cit., pp. 258-92.

[6]M.B. Emeneau, 'The Non-Literary Dravidian Languages', in Norman H. Zide, ed., *Current Trends in Linguistics,* vol. V, *Linguistics in South Asia,* Mouton, The Hague, 1969, pp. 334-42.

which may be related to Proto-Dravidian.[7]

The mid-Ganga plains retain several small Dravidian pockets till today. Dhāṅgar, which is a dialect of Dravidian Kurukh language spoken by the Oraons in Chotanagpur, is present in the *terai* districts of Nepal,[8] which form an extension of the mid-Ganga plains towards the Himalayas. This Dravidian dialect is also spoken by the Dhāṅgar tribe in Madhubani and Western Champaran districts of north Bihar. In course of time the Dhāṅgar tribe appears as a caste, and at present its members are landless labourers employed in agriculture and well-digging. Although this caste is found only in a few villages, Dhāṅgar is used as a pejorative term by the upper castes for those who are condemned as uncultured. It is significant that in Hindi dictionaries Dhāṅgar is called a non-Aryan caste.[9] Besides Dhāṅgar, Malto, another Dravidian dialect closely related to Kurukh, is spoken in the Rajmahal hills lying at the eastern end of the mid-Ganga zone.[10]

There is no basis for the view that the Dravidian substratum of the Indo-Aryan languages is absent in Pakistan, Rajasthan, Haryana, Punjab and northern parts

[7]Braj Kachru, 'Kashmiri and Other Dardic Languages', in Zide, ed., op. cit., pp. 284-306.

[8]Kent H. Gordon and Kenneth L. Pike, 'Paired Semantic Components, Paired Sentence Reversals and the Analysis of Dhāṅgar-Kudux Discourse', in Ronald Trail, *Patterns in Clause, Sentence and Discourse in selected Languages of India and Nepal,* pt I, Sentence and Discourse, Summer Institute of Linguistics of the University of Okalahama, Norman, 1973, p. 341, fn. 1; also see Introduction, p. 1. Dhāṅgar is also called Dhāṅgarī.

[9]S.V. Dhāṅgar, Kalika Prasad et al., eds., *Vṛhat Hindī Kośa;* Ramchandra Verma, ed., *Saṃkṣipta Hindī Śabdasāgara,* Nagari-pracharini Sabha, Kashi, 1987.

[10]M.S. Andronov, *Dravidian Languages,* p. 23; Malto is also called Maler.

of Uttar Pradesh.[11] As shown earlier, the Dravidian language Brahui is spoken in Sind and Baluchistan. Further, quite a few Dravidian agricultural terms occur in Hindi-speaking areas[12] including Uttar Pradesh and some of them also appear in Punjabi and Haryanavi. Turner notes a good many Dravidian words in the Indo-Aryan languages. These include *kākka* or *kākā* (uncle), *kulatha* (a kind of pulse), *kulāla* (potter), *kuṇḍa* (pot), *kuṇḍala* (ear-ring) and *gaṇḍa* (cheek).[13] He also points out some Munda words including *gaṇḍa* (rhinocerous), *lāṅgala* (plough) and *lāṅgula* (tail) in these languages.[14] Some non-Aryan words may have been borrowed later, but many of them were adopted when the Indo-Aryan first confronted the pre-Aryan languages. Thus there is fairly strong evidence for the presence of the pre-Aryan stratum in the Indo-Aryan languages. Some borrowed words suggest that pre-Aryan agricultural and pot-making practices influenced the Indo-Aryans.

We may add that some Dravidian kinship terms appear in Gujarat and Maharashtra.[15] Trautmann postulates a Dravidian presence all along the west coast up to and including Kathiawar.[16] According to McAlpin, the pattern of the distirbution of Dravidian languages supports

[11]B.B. Lal, *India 1947-1997: New Light on the Indus Civilization*, Aryan Books International, New Delhi, 1998, pp. 118-19.

[12]Colin P. Mosica, 'Aryan and Non-Aryan Elements in North Indian Agriculture', in M.M. Deshpande and P.E. Hook, eds., *Aryan and Non-Aryan in India,* University of Michigan, Ann Arbor, 1979, pp. 55-151, esp. 76-102.

[13]Turner, op. cit., nos. 2998, 3264, 3268, 3335, 3341, and 3999.

[14]Ibid., nos. 4000, 11006 and 11009.

[15]Thomas R. Trautmann, 'The Study of Dravidian Kinship', in Deshpande and Hook, eds., op. cit., p. 164.

[16]Ibid.

the concept of a fairly recent expansion of Dravidian into the Indian peninsula through Gujarat with possible forerunners.[17] Further, Trautmann supports Southworth's view that Marathi and Mahārāṣṭrī Prakrit developed in an ancient Maharashtrian population which was Dravidian in speech. Southworth suggests that both Dravidian and Indo-Aryan derived floral terms from the language of older inhabitants.[18] Whether this earlier substratum is represented by some Austric or other language can be substantiated only by future research. At any rate the survival of Dravidian terms and dialects suggest the spread of Dravidian in ancient times in a major part of the northern subcontinent.

Lal asks for the Harappan material remains in the areas associated with the Dravidian language,[19] but they can be seen at several places. As shown by McAlpin, the Dravidians went to the south via Gujarat. So this region has numerous Harappan sites which lasted longer than in the north. Some of them continued till 1400 BC and even 800 BC.[20] Probably the Dravidians also passed through western Maharashtra, and so Harappan influence appears at Daimabad and a few other places. However, the Dravidians reached the south relatively late in the second millennium BC[21] when the Harappan culture had become extinct. Naturally its remains are not found in that region.

[17] David W. McAlpin, op. cit., in Deshpande and Hook, eds., op. cit., p. 182.

[18] Franklin C. Southworth, 'Lexical Evidence for Early Contacts between Indo-Aryan and Dravidian', in Deshpande and Hook, eds., op. cit., p. 206.

[19] B.B. Lal, 1998, op. cit., p. 118.

[20] M.K. Dhavalikar, *Cultural Imperialism (Indus Civilization in Western India)*, Books & Books, New Delhi, 1995, p. 48.

[21] McAlpin, 'Linguistic Prehistory: The Dravidian Situation', in Deshpande and Hook, eds., op. cit., p. 182.

Spread of the Indo-Aryan speech

In the long run the people of the Indus valley, Iran, Afghanistan, Baluchistan, NWF Province, Kashmir and parts of the Ganga zone adopted the Indo-Aryan speech. The spread of the speech is suggested by the existing recension of the *Ṛg Veda* which contains twenty-five Dravidian loans. Several linguists including Burrow and Deshpande point out phonetic changes in Proto-Aryan letters under Dravidian influence.[22] It is held that retroflexion in the existing *Ṛg Veda* is an indication of pre-Vedic Dravidization of the Aryan language.[23] The letters *ṭa, ṭha, ḍa,* etc., are considered Dravidian contribution to the Indo-Aryan alphabet. Notably enough, we find only a few entries under them in Sanskrit dictionaries. The *Ṛg Veda* seems to have been composed by a Sanskritist who was familiar with the Dravidian language. Since archaeological data do not support the Aryan conquest of Harappa the spread of the Aryan language in this area cannot be confidently attributed to this factor. However, Parpola places the continuous struggles of the Aryans with the Dāsas and Dasyus in Bactria and Margiana where he notices the type of structure described in the *Ṛg Veda*.[24] Thus the Indo-Aryan domination may have spread their language in north Afghanistan and south-east Turkmenistan. Shaffer suggests that 'extensive trading networks' led to the spread of the Aryan language,[25] but also holds that the

[22]Madhav M. Deshpande, 'Vedic Aryans, non-Vedic Aryans, and non-Aryans: Judging the linguistic evidence of the Veda', in Erdosy, ed., op. cit., pp. 67-84.

[23]Ibid., pp. 76-7.

[24]Asko Parpola, 'The Problem of the Aryans and the Soma: Textual-linguistic and archaeological evidence', in George Erdosy, ed., op. cit., pp. 367-8.

[25]Shaffer in Luckas, ed., op. cit., pp. 86-7.

Harappan culture was not involved to any great extent with the international trade of the third millennium BC.[26] This is all the more true of the pastoral and agricultural tribes of Central Asia in the second millennium BC. Archaeology does not know of widespread trade networks in this period. Even in the industrial stage language diffusion through such networks is confined to small, upper sections of society. Similarly, missionary activities cannot explain the spread of language on any scale in this period or any part of the pre-industrial era. In the late eighteenth century nineteen languages were spoken in New York. How English became the dominant language and the only official language of the USA is a good subject for working out a model for the spread and dominance of a language. Meanwhile we can consider Renfrew's view on this problem. According to him a language spreads because of elite dominance and more productive mode of subsistence.[27] This view is broadly supported by modern examples. The social dominance and numerical strength of the Bengali-speaking people in Purulia district led its Kurmi tribals to give up Kurmali and adopt Bengali.[28] It is clear that the use of the horse, war chariot, spoked wheels, cheek pieces for the horse, and numerous weapons which all appear in the Sintashta cemetery and in the Bactria-Margiana Archaeological Complex (BMAC), gave a distinct technological advantage to the Indo-Iranians. Combined with the rituals of the fire cult, *soma* cult and cremation this advantage ensured the social dominance of the Indo-Aryan chiefs and priests.

But how could the language of the Indo-Aryans spread in the subcontinent without their coming

[26]Ibid.

[27]Renfrew, op. cit.

[28]Finding based on my field-work in Manbhum district in 1948.

here? The scale of linguistic diffusion in India presupposes the presence of large numbers of Indo-Aryan speakers. If invasion and massive migrations in two or three waves are ruled out, we have to think of intermittent immigrations for centuries. It is clear that 'a goal-oriented subgroup' of 'people migrates, not culture'.[29] This is especially true of the spread of a language in the pre-industrial stage, particularly in prehistoric times. It would be a miracle if the Indo-Aryan language spread in India without the arrival of a good many speakers. But what can we do if some archaeologists believe in miracles?

Aryan elements in late and post-Harappan cultures of the north

S.R. Rao, a proponent of the Aryan homeland in India, significantly notes that the duration of the late Harappan period in Kutch, Rajasthan, Haryana, Punjab, Jammu & Kashmir was shorter than in Saurashtra and north Gujarat.[30] Thus the late Harappans survived longer in the south than in the north.[31] This difference can be attributed to the rise of new cultures in the northern part of the subcontinent and the spread of the late Harappan culture in its western part. But all the new cultures may not belong to the Aryan-speaking peoples. According to Mackay, the Jhangar and Jhukar cultures bridge the dark period between

[29]David W. Anthony, 'Migration in Archaeology: The Baby and the Bathwater', *American Anthropology*, vol. 92, no. 4, 1990, p. 906.

[30]'New Light on the Post-Urban/Late Harappan Phase of the Indus Civilization in India', in G. Possehl, ed., *Harappan Civilization: A Contemporary Perspective*, 1982, p. 358.

[31]S. Manik and S.A. Chanchal, *The Aryans and the Indus Civilization*, Dinratri Prakashan, Dhaka, 1995, p. 13.

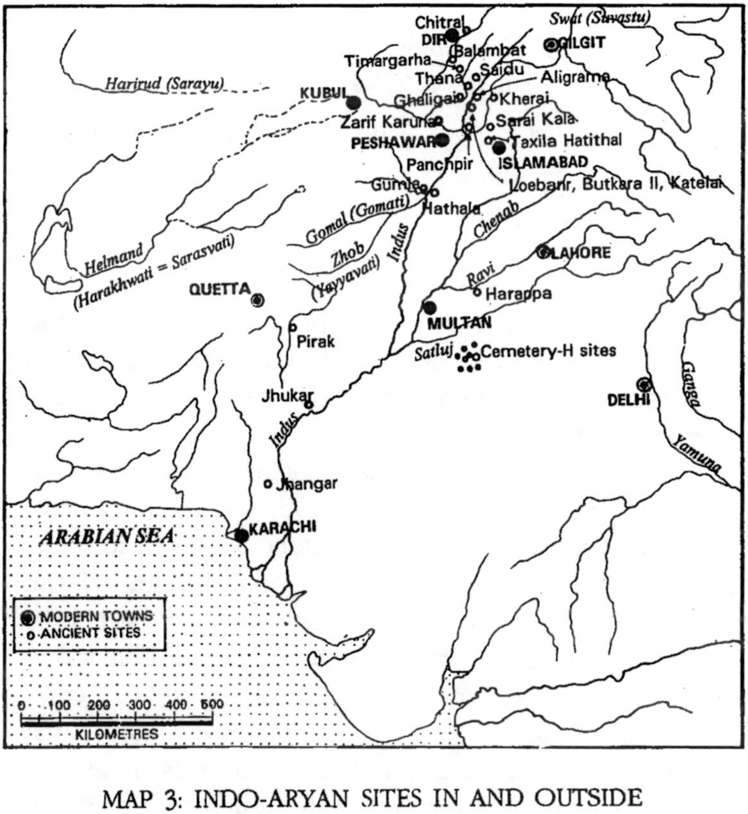

MAP 3: INDO-ARYAN SITES IN AND OUTSIDE RG VEDIC RIVER VALLEY.

the desertion of the Harappa sites and the coming of the Aryan-speaking people around 1500 BC. The Jhukar people used seals and pottery quite different from those of the Harappa folk. The possibility of their being 'the fore-runners of the Aryan invaders has to be considered'.[32]

Archaeology of the Aryan arrival in India

The stage of the Aryan advent in the subcontinent covers Periano Ghundai on the Zhob river in north Baluchistan, Pirak near the Bolan pass, Gumla and other grave sites near the Gomal pass in the Gomal valley, and Gandhara grave sites in the Swat valley. All the sites lie in the border area of the subcontinent. They show the use of the horse and the practice of cremation, which recalls the Fedorovo type of cremation in the Andronovo culture of north Central Asia.[33]

Of these sites we may first mention Periano Ghundai overlooking the river Zhob, a western tributary of the Indus. The site shows habitation around 2000 BC, and its occupants buried the cremated remains of the dead in tall urns, right in the houses. They also used horse which appears in a terracotta figure. Sankalia thinks that considerable Iranian and Harappan features appear here.[34] Moreover, at Moghal Ghundai in the Zhob valley burial cairns have produced a tripod-jar, horse-bells, rings and bangles which are compared to the equipment of about 1000 BC from 'Cemetery-B'at Sialk in central Iran, but may

[32]Ernest Mackay, op. cit., pp. xi, 4, 5, 114, 126, 154 and 157.

[33]Parpola in Erdosy, ed., pp. 357-66.

[34]*Ṛ*V, VI. 27.6; Sankalia, p. 324.

be later.[35] We may note that the river Zhob is identical with the Yavyāvatī of the *Ṛg Veda* and Indra with his two red steads is said to have destroyed three thousand warriors in a tribal war on this river.[36] The term *yavyāvatī* denotes streamlet, and is used in this sense in several Dardic dialects.[37] This suggests that from the Zhob valley the early Vedic people spread to North-West Frontier Province.

Pirak near the Bolan pass is another site in Baluchistan where terracotta models of horses and Bactrian camels appear in 1800-1700 BC. They show a marked break with the Harappan style, and according to Jarrige may indicate a major folk intrusion from the north, from Bactria-Margiana.[38] The presence of birch wood houses in Pirak remind us of similar houses in the Andronovo sites of Central Asia. It is well known that the Sanskrit *bhūrja*, which stands for birch, has its cognates in several Indo-European languages.

The Swat region is known to archaeologists as the seat of the Gandhara grave culture, which emerged around the seventeenth century BC. Gandhara is mentioned in later Vedic texts, but the Swat represents the early Vedic Suvāstu on the bank of which the Ṛg Vedic King Trasadasyu made liberal gifts. This 'frightener of the Dasyus' is called an *arya* which is interpreted as *svāmī* by Sāyaṇa. Besides the presence of the *arya* Trasadasyu, the ford of the Suvāstu shows a brown chariot and a horse.[39] From 1300 BC onwards its valley provides a good many instances of post-

[35]Wheeler, op. cit., p. 133.

[36]*ṚV*, XXVII.5-7; The gist given above is on the basis of Sāyaṇa's commentary and Griffith's translation.

[37]Turner, op. cit., no. 10442.

[38]Bridget Allchin and Raymond Allchin, *Origins of a Civilization, The Prehistory and Early Archaeology of South Asia*, Viking, New Delhi, 1997, p. 213.

[39]*ṚV*, VIII. 19. 36-7.

cremation burials containing horse remains and furnishings. It also shows a few settlements. People lived on the hills and their slopes, not far away from the river banks. Interestingly enough, we notice quite a few pit-dwellings[40] which remind us of the *garta* or the house in the *Ṛg Veda*.[41] The people also built houses of stone which may have something to do with the *guhā*. This term is generally translated by Griffith as cave, cavern, secret place, sacred cell, hidden, concealed and dwelling place—on the basis of the commentary of Sāyaṇa, who also takes it to be a sacrificial place. But the term may indicate both stone house and pit-dwelling, which characterize the Gomal and Gandhara people. The Ghaligai excavations in the Swat valley show rock shelters whose calibrated dates range from *c.* 3000 BC to 1700 BC. These shelters are called 'favoured locations for pastoral nomad camps which may account for discontinuities noted at Ghaligai'.[42] It seems that the frequent use of the Ṛg Vedic *guhā* in which the Vedic deities and cattle lived indicates these rock shelters as well as stone houses found in the Swat and Gomal valleys.[43] The stone 'forts' (*aśman* or *aśmanmayī purs*) of the *Ṛg Veda*[44] may also stand for stone houses and rock shelters of the Swat and Gomal valleys.

Again, from Loebanr III in the Swat valley large oval pit house and storage pits are compared to Burzahom pit-houses and those found in the eastern Tibetan Plateau and north-eastern China.[45] The use of the Burzahom pit dwellings has been explained in the light of the *Ṛg*

[40]Dani in Dani and Masson, eds., op. cit., pp. 404, 413.
[41]*s.v. garta*, Monier-Williams, *SED*.
[42]Shaffer, op. cit., pp. 433, 446.
[43]Dani in Dani and Masson, eds., op. cit., p. 403.
[44]Rau, 1976, op. cit., pp. 26-7.
[45]Shaffer, op. cit., pp. 437, 446.

Veda.[46] The term *garta* used in the early portions of the *Ṛg Veda* indicates a pit-dwelling. The neolithic Burzahom also shows burnt birch which could be the remains of a roof destroyed by fire.[47] Sankalia suggests that the neolithic people came here from outside, and the Allchins connect them with north China or Central Asia.[48] Birch and pit-dwelling may be Aryan, but horse and other important Aryan traits are absent. Since the calibrated date for the concerned layers is around 2500 BC,[49] perhaps they indicate the influence of the Afanasievo culture which is associated with the speakers of the western branch of the Indo-European language in the Altai zone. It seems that it touched the Chinese borders lying in the north-east of the Pamirs. In the Burzahom context the Kunal pit-dwelling in Haryana may also be examined.

Pit-dwellings were known to the horse using pastoralists as early as the fifth millennium BC.[50] Later from the fourth to the second millennium BC there is clear and considerable evidence for subterranean houses in Russia[51] and Central Asia. In the Andronovo culture of the second millennium BC in Central Asia birch wood was used in the construction of these houses.[52] Therefore either the Indo-

[46]R.N. Nandi, 'Aryan Settlements and the Rgveda', *Indian Historical Review*, vol. XXI, nos. 1-2, July 1994/January 1995, pp. 18-19.

[47]*Indian Archaeology 1961-62: A Review*, p. 17; cf. M. Sharif and B.K. Thapar, 'Food-producing communities in Pakistan and northern India', in Dani and Masson, eds., op. cit., pp. 138-51.

[48]*The Birth of Indian Civilization*, 1968, p. 160.

[49]Gregory L. Possehl, 'Radiocarbon Dates for South Asian Archaeology', University Museum, University of Pennsylvania, Philadelphia, June 1989 (cyclostyled copy), calibration 2, pp. 11-12.

[50]J.P. Mallory, *In Search of the Indo-Europeans*, p. 198.

[51]Ibid., p. 211.

[52]Ibid., pp. 228-9.

Aryans introduced pit-dwelling in the Swat valley or they easily adopted the practice with which they had been familiar.

Clearly, the Gomal and Gandhara people did not use fired bricks, and their pots suggest a rural setting.[53] Thus the Swat settlers may have been the earliest speakers of the Indo-Aryan language in the subcontinent. According to Stacul, the Swat cultural complex of about 1500 BC marked by northern Iranian influences 'very probably shows a transitional phase between the Harappan culture and Cemetery-H',[54] which announces the coming of a new people.

The material from the Swat cemeteries is considered closely related to Iran and the Caucasus. The Allchins think that the grave sites had a 'thoroughly Iranian equipment'.[55] But according to E.E. Kuzmina the Swat material has its counterpart in the cemeteries of south Tajikistan in 1500-1000 BC.[56] Probably both of them were derived from the same source. In any case the Gandhara grave culture does not appear to be a purely local product. Neither the use of horse nor the practice of cremation appears to be a local phenomenon. Even pit-dwelling may not have been a purely local feature because it appears in the undifferentiated Yamnya culture of the Indo-Europeans and also in the Andronovo culture associated with the Proto-Indians and Proto-Iranians. The Yamnya culture

[53]Dani in Dani and Masson, op. cit., pp. 415-16.

[54]Giorgio Stacul, 'Harappan Post-urban Evidence in the Swat Valley', in B.B. Lal and S.P. Gupta, eds., *Frontiers of the Indus Civilization*, Books & Books, New Delhi, 1984, pp. 271-5.

[55]Bridget Allchin and Raymond Allchin, *The Birth of Indian Civilization*, Penguin, Harmondsworth, 1968, p. 152.

[56]B.A. Litvinsky and L.T. Pyankova in Dani and Masson, eds., op. cit., p. 393.

existed in the Volga-Ural region in the fourth and third millennia BC, and the Andronovo culture covered almost the whole of Central Asia in the second millennium BC. The two cultures are considered to be the progenitors of the Indo-Aryan culture.

Several sites exposed in the Gomal valley show burnt material in lower and earlier graves, and the grave in this valley is called a burial as well as a funeral pyre. Inside the grave the funerary material includes horses and hubbed wheels.[57] According to Sankalia, the Harappan culture of Gumla 'was destroyed by fire and a fight in which sling balls and terracotta missiles were also used'.[58] Dani is convinced that the grave culture people destroyed the Harappan culture of the Gumla site,[59] which lies on the Indus and is not far from the Gomal valley. Significantly, the Gomal, a western tributary of the Indus, is identical with the Gomati river which is associated in the *Ṛg Veda* with an Aryan chieftain.[60] All the grave cultures exhibit striking exotic features such as the use of the horse and cremation, but they may also have local elements such as rock-shelter dwellings.

Lying in the geographical area of the *Ṛg Veda*, Cemetery-H and Pirak show traits of Aryan culture. More importantly, similar sites appear in the valleys of the Ṛg Vedic rivers Suvāstu (Swat), Gomatī (Gomal) and Yavyāvatī (Zhob). All these sites found in the river valleys or outside furnish adequate archaeological data to establish the arrival of the Ṛg Vedic people in the first half of second millennium BC.

[57]Dani in Dani and Masson, eds., op. cit., pp. 400-1.
[58]Sankalia, op. cit., p. 330.
[59]Ibid.
[60]XXIV. 27-30.

Nature of biological evidence

Although the Gandhara grave culture has been called Aryan by Dani and Vedic by Erdosy, there is difference of opinion about the identity of skeletons buried in its graves. In our view the real issue is not to identify the 'Aryan' skeleton but to look for unfamiliar skeletons and ethnic pluralism. Dani approvingly quotes the finding of Bernhardt, who examined twenty-five skulls from Gandhara and found the most common type to be the Mediterranean type including its subtypes, such as the Transcaspian or the Khorasan.[61] In his opinion the human remains are closely similar to crania from the Caucasus, the Volga region and Tepe Hissar in north-east Iran.[62]

However, a team of biological anthropologists consisting of Hemphill, Lukacs and Kennedy notices significant similarities between Harappan and Gandharan human remains[63] and rules out the presence of any outside element. This team compares the Gandhara material with crania from Egypt, Anatolia, Mesopotamia and the Iranian plateau. But it leaves out Central Asia and Eastern Europe including Russia; apparently it does not visualize any possibility of migration from these regions towards India. Further, it does not detect any serious flaw in the method of Bernhardt.

However, Kennedy states that individual samples from Timargarha, open burials of Cemetery-H and of Cemetery-R 37 show 'closest affinities to individuals from Tepe Hissar III'.[64] The Hissar evidence given by Kennedy reinforces the finding of Bernhardt regarding similarity

[61]Dani in Dani and Masson, eds., op. cit., p. 407.
[62]Kenneth A.R. Kennedy in Erdosy, ed., op. cit., p. 49.
[63]Ibid.
[64]Ibid.

between the Hissar and the Gandhara crania. This would suggest that either people from north-east Iran went to north-western India around 1900-1800 BC, or the same set of tribes migrated to both Iran and India from a common habitation. In any case it would undermine the basic finding of the team that demographic discontinuities appear only twice, once between 6000 BC and 4500 BC and again after 800 BC. The second discontinuity supports the view that the speakers of the Indo-Aryan languages came in successive groups and also ties up with the theory of dramatic change in climate at the advent of the first millennium BC. Examination of more data might provide more examples of demographic discontinuities in the first half of the second millennium BC.

Kennedy asks for biological criteria for Aryanness. But if an archaeological culture shows Aryan features it need not be attributed to a homogenous ethnic group. It is well known that the skeletons of the Harappans do not belong to one single ethnic group. This may also apply to the Vedic or Aryan culture, which may show ethnic pluralism. The physical features of the Bihari immigrants in East Bengal (Bangladesh) change in the third/fourth generation on account of climatic conditions. Does such a factor also influence the Indo-Aryans? Therefore it is better to investigate the periodwise territorial and cultural connections of the Indo-Aryans than to get entangled in the issue of their ethnic identity.

At any rate, the evidence provided by Bernhardt clearly confirms migration to the borders of the subcontinent of a people who used horses, practised cremation and spoke the Vedic language. In Vats' view an elaborate painting on a burial pot recalls cremation rites, ritual and beliefs found in hymns 14, 16 and 18 of the tenth

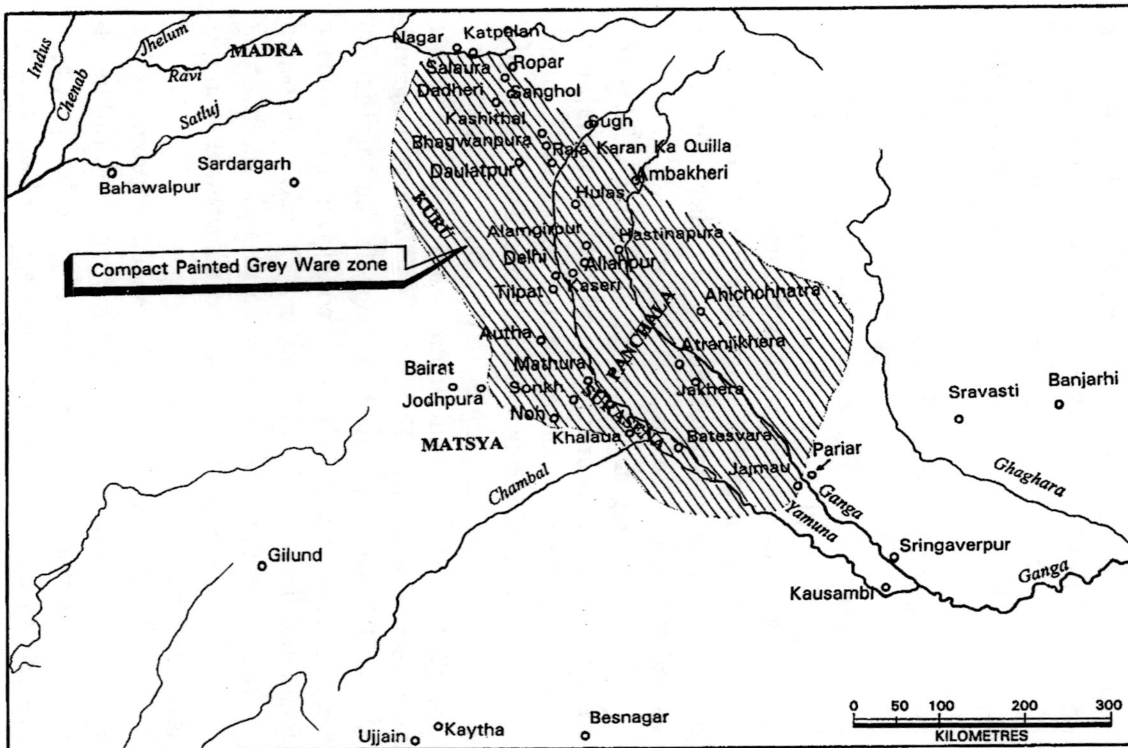

MAP 4: PAINTED GREY WARE AREA.

maṇḍala of the *Ṛg Veda.*[65] He adds that since the paintings are connected with post-exposure fractional burials and not with cremation the comparison cannot be carried further.[66]

But the fractional burials of the later period in Cemetery-H also show pieces of burnt bones. These occur along with the skull and a few large bones deposited in large urns.[67] This indicates partial cremation practised by some Cemetery-H people. Therefore Vats notices 'a radical difference between earth burials, complete or fractional, of the IInd stratum, and the post-exposure pot-burials of the top stratum', and attributes this to foreign immigration.[68] The Allchins suggest an early Indo-Iranian wave in the Cemetery-H area because the Iranian sites show the same painted patterns as occur in the Cemetery-H pottery.[69] The similarity may be due to the presence of the same subgroup of Aryans in both the Iranian and Cemetery-H sites.

Archaeological stages in Aryan expansion in north India

The graves in the villages of the Swat, Gomal and Zhob along with Cemetery-H sites and the Pirak complex announce the arrival of the Aryans in the second millennium BC. This coming coincides with the climatic change in Central Asia during the same period. The second stage of the Aryan advance covers Punjab, Haryana and western U.P. It heralds the advent of iron and the Painted

[65]M.S. Vats, *Excavations at Harappa*, vol. I, p. 234.
[66]Ibid., p. 209.
[67]Dani in Dani and Masson, eds., op. cit., p. 399.
[68]M.S. Vats, op. cit., p. 234.
[69]Allchins, 1968, op. cit., pp. 149, 314.

Grey Ware culture. Nearly 750 PGW sites have been located. According to Vibha Tripathi, except for the paste, the PGW is not different from the Pirak pottery.[70]

I have shown that the material culture of the later Vedic texts is reflected in the PGW culture.[71] Some of its faunal and floral features such as the presence of the elephant and rice remind us of earlier times when the area was forested and rainy. There may have been other indigenous elements in the PGW culture. Although the PGW is nearly similar to the Pirak pottery, its examples do not occur in Afghanistan, Central Asia, Iran and Turkey.[72] Hence it cannot be considered an early Aryan pottery from outside. It would be absurd to think that the immigrants carried the whole set of their fauna, flora, crockery and implements. Most probably the Aryans adopted the Grey Ware prevalent in south Central Asia and its neighbourhood. Grey gritty ware and black-burnished grey ware formed the two main wares out of the three found in the Swat sites of about 1500 BC.[73] It seems that the Aryans eventually refined the Grey Ware into the PGW. The hilly connection of the PGW people may be inferred from their use of the *chīr* wood in the Ganga plains.[74] It is also significant that the PGW shows the svastika first found in Elam and later in Baluchistan, Central Asia and Harappan sites. More importantly, the PGW sites do show horse remains, fire

[70]Vibha Tripathi, *The Painted Grey Ware: An Iron Age Culture of Northern India*, Concept Publishing, Delhi, 1976.

[71]Sharma, *Material Culture and Social Formations in Ancient India*, Chap. IV.

[72]A. Ghosh qoted in V.D. Misra, op. cit., pp. 15, 23; cf. Sharma, *Looking for the Aryans*, p. 12.

[73]Stacul, 1984, pp. 271-5.

[74]B.B. Lal. 'The Painted Grey Ware Culture of the Iron Age', in Dani and Masson, eds., op. cit., pp. 425-6.

altars and also indicate cremation. Bhagwanpura, Dadheri, Nagar and Katpalan are good examples.[75]

The mid-Ganga plains show the third stage of Aryan expansion, which is marked by the Black Slipped Ware and Northern Black Polished Ware culture, and is noted for effective use of iron tools in production. The later Vedic people moved towards the east and so did the PGW and the BSW with them. The NBPW seems to have emerged out of the PGW and BSW.[76] All these three ceramics show a complete break with the Harappan tradition of pottery.

[75]J.P. Joshi, *Excavation at Bhagwanpura: 1975-76*, ASI, Govt. of India, New Delhi, 1993.

[76]Sharma, *The State and Varna Formation in the Mid-Ganga Plains: An Ethnoarchaeological View*, Manohar, New Delhi, 1996.

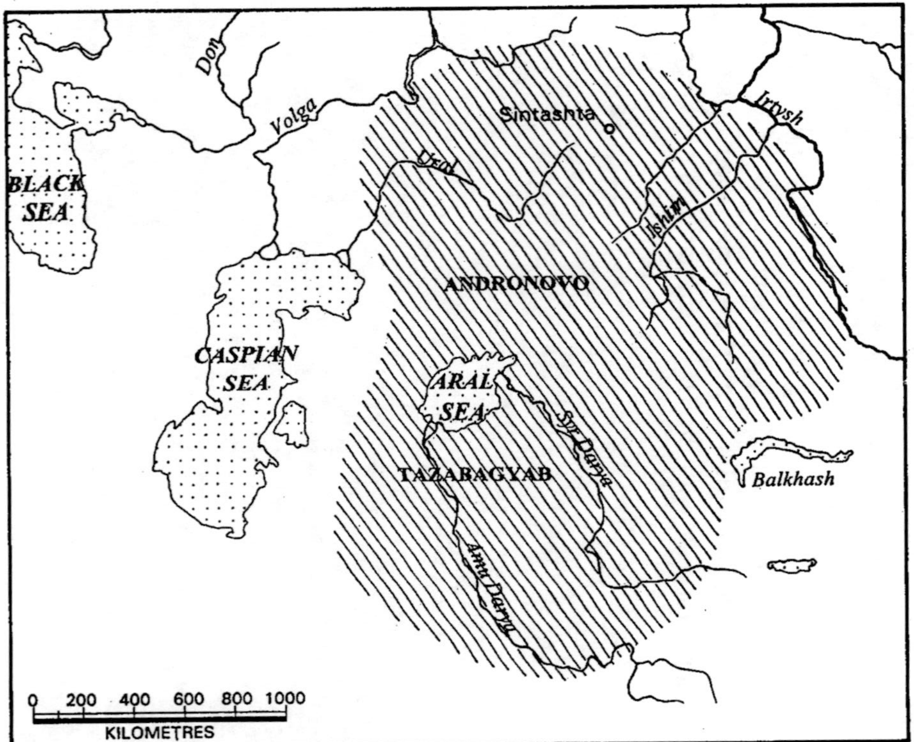

MAP 5: AREA OF THE ANDRONOVO CULTURE.

CHAPTER 4

Migration from Central Asia

Central Asian cultures and the Indo-Aryans

Central Asia may not be the original home of the Indo-Europeans, but it provided an intermediate home for the Indo-Iranians comprising the Proto-Indo-Aryans and the Proto-Indo-Iranians. Their material life is reflected in the Andronovo culture, which is named after the type site at the village of Andrŏnovo situated in the middle reaches of the Yenisey in southern Siberia.[1] The Bronze Age steppe culture of the second millennium BC shows striking traits of the Indo-Aryan life. The 'Andronovo culture' is a blanket term for several related cultures which covered nearly 3000 km from the Urals through Kazakhstan to western Siberia, and from the forest steppe in north Central Asia to Tajikistan in south Central Asia. Several Russian archaeologists suggest that the Andronovo culture was the counterpart of the material culture common to the *Ṛg Veda* and the *Avesta*.[2]

[1]Alexander Mongait, *Archaeology in the U.S.S.R.*, Foreign Languages Publishing House, Moscow, 1959, pp. 144-6.

[2]Y.Y. Kuzmina and K.F. Smirnov, 'The Origin of the Indo-Iranians in the Light of Recent Archaeological Data', *Journal of Central Asia*, vol. 1, no. 1, 1978, pp. 68-70; J.P. Mallory, op. cit., pp. 228-9.

The remains of the culture scattered from western Kazakhstan to the middle Yenisey river show that the people reared goat, sheep, cattle and horse, and horses accounted for about a third of the livestock. A cemetery at the bank of the Sintashta shows that in the lands along the east of the south Urals and west of Kazakhstan horse-drawn war chariots with ten spoked wheels were used. They also used cheek pieces and probably spikes for the horses. It seems that the charioteers formed an important social class. People lived on stock-breeding and agriculture. They also observed the cult of the *soma* drink, and used svastika motifs on their vessels. They also performed the horse sacrifice. Hence they are called a part of the Indo-Iranian tribes who appeared around 1700 BC.[3] On the Ob and Yenisey rivers in the eastern region both burial and cremation were in vogue. Cremation was known in northern and eastern Kazakhstan, and was dominant in the Urals and southern Kazakhstan.[4]

Though people practised farming, stock-breeding was far more important in their economy. They lived in rectangular pit-dwellings, whose roofs rested on posts. In one case close to their settlement they had a place for sacrifice where clay pots were kept in holes. Some holes show charred domestic animal bones together with wheat stalks and seeds.[5] This suggests that animals were burnt in sacrifices.

While south Central Asia was inhabited by farmers and had developed elements of proto-urbanism, north Central Asia was mainly a steppe zone peopled by

[3]V.F. Gening, 'The Cemetery at Sintashta and the Early Indo-Iranian Peoples', *JIES*, vol. 7, nos. 3 and 4, 1979, p. 29.

[4]Parpola in Erdosy, ed., op. cit., p. 357.

[5]Mongait, op. cit., p. 146.

pastoral groups. In the arid and semi-desert steppe zone, the pastorals practised transhumance and in the cold and dry season moved to the western part of south Tajikistan because of its warm, mild and moist climate. Eventually many of them settled in this area. According to Masson, 'the movement of the steppe bronze tribes far southwards right up to the middle reaches of the Amu Darya is indisputable'.[6] According to Fairservice, the pastoralists who moved to the Indian borderlands came from Bactria-Margiana Archaeological Complex or the BMAC which saw the genesis of the culture of the *Ṛg Veda.*[7]

The BMAC roughly includes south Turkmenistan, northern Afghanistan and part of south Uzbekistan. In 1900-1500 BC, it shows the presence of the horse, spoked wheels, *soma* drink cult, fire cult and cremation.[8] From here people migrated to south-eastern Iran, southern Afghanistan, Gandhara and the Quetta regions. Hiebert, a strong champion of the theory of local cultural tradition, doubts massive population movements. However, burial assemblages including artefacts and ceramics suggest to him the movement of the people from the oases of both Bactria and Margiana to the periphery of the Indus valley. He hesitates to associate with the movement the introduction of the Indo-Iranian languages, which seems to imply both Indo-Iranian and Indo-Aryan speeches.[9]

Stacul notices similarity between the black-

[6]Masson in Dani and Masson, eds., op. cit., pp. 347-56.

[7]Walter A. Fairservice (Jr.), 'Central Asia and the Ṛgveda: The archaeological evidence', in George Erdosy, ed., op. cit., pp. 206-12.

[8]Parpola in Erdosy, ed., op. cit., pp. 366-74; R.S. Sharma, *Looking for the Aryans*, p. 49.

[9]Fredrik T. Hiebert, 'South Asia from a Central Asian Perspective', in George Erdosy, ed., op. cit., pp. 200-2.

burnished grey ware of the Swat valley and that of north Iran. Further, he compares several other ware types of the valley including the black-burnished grey ware, with those from Dashly in north Afghanistan. According to him the Dashly pottery has affinities with that from Shah Tepe, Tepe Hissar and Tureng Tepe in Iran. Since the black-burnished grey ware is as old as 2500 BC,[10] all this implies migration from north Iran and north Afghanistan to the Swat valley. Stacul also notices in the valley pottery paintings and considers them similar to those from the north Iranian plateau. He speaks of a cultural wave from north Iran to the valley, and attributes the paintings to long-range trade. But a horse representation on a potsherd from Bir-kot-ghundai in the Swat valley is dated 1700-1400 BC and considered by him 'obviously of great significance in terms of migrations'.[11]

Stacul's findings suggest earlier cultural waves from Iran and Afghanistan in the Swat valley before 2000 BC. But the horse depiction on the potsherd may be connected with the horse-using people in the Andronovo culture. Elena Kuzmina points out parallels in both the domestic architecture and burial rites of the Gandhara grave culture and the regional variants of the Andronovans to the north.[12] We also learn that the ceramics of Dashly Tepe (north Afghanistan) and Sapalli Tepe (south Uzbekistan) provide better analogies for the type of the pottery we find in the Gandhara grave culture.[13] This

[10]Giorgio Stacul, *Prehistoric and Protohistoric Swat, Pakistan (c. 3000-1400 BC)*, Rome, ISMEO, 1987, p. 122.

[11]Stacul, 'Harappan Post-urban Evidence in the Swat Valley', in B.B. Lal and S.P. Gupta, eds., op. cit., pp. 271-5.

[12]J.P. Mallory, *In Search of the Indo-Europeans*, p. 230.

[13]Ibid., p. 231.

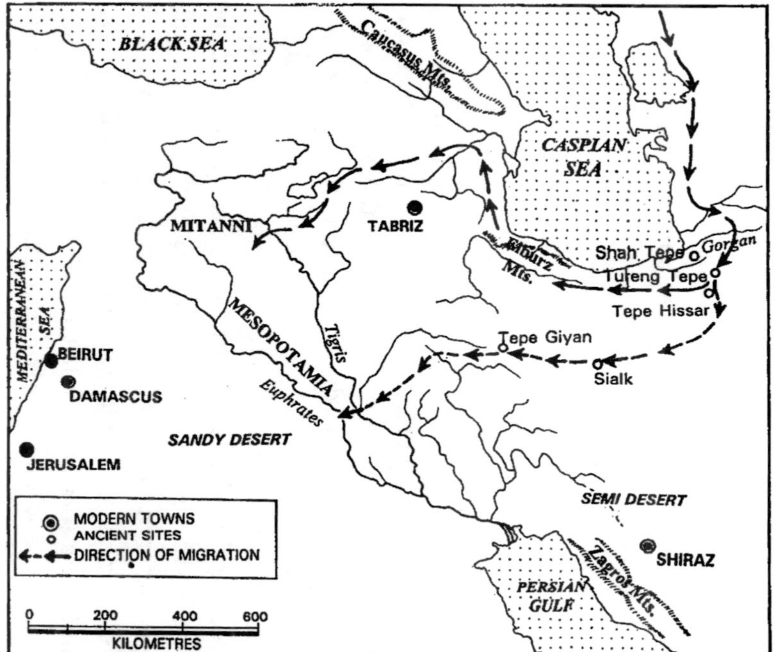

MAP 6: INDO ARYAN MIGRATION ROUTES FROM CENTRAL ASIA TO MESOPOTAMIA.

indicates the impact of migration of the BMAC people on the Swat valley.

Causes of migration from Central Asia

Important elements of culture found in Cemetery-H, Pirak, the Zhob, Gomal and the Swat valleys in the second millennium BC were introduced by the immigrants from Central Asia. Climatic change was the main cause of their migration. Many paleo-climatists hold that extreme aridity and freezing-point conditions prevailed in Central Asia in the late third and early second millennia BC.[14] According to Khazanov 'the second millennium BC was characterised by dry climate which, it would appear, was at its driest at the turn of the second and the first millennium BC. Archaeological data would confirm this suggestion.'[15] Evidently bitter cold and dry climate turned the agriculturists mainly into pastoralists and forced them to migrate to warmer and rainy regions. Adequate archaeological evidence has been adduced to demonstrate the movements of the semi-nomadic peoples in Central Asia in the second millennium BC and at the turn of the first millennium BC.[16] The movement of cattle and other pastoralists is also attributed to a social and political schism in the second millennium BC between the urban elite and cattle pastoralists. This is the view of Fairservice who considers the Ṛg Vedic

[14]Masson in Dani and Masson, eds., op. cit., pp. 43-4.

[15]A.M. Khazanov, *Nomadism and the Outside World*, Cambridge University Press, 1984, p. 95, quoted in M.K. Dhavalikar, *Cultural Imperialism (Indus Civilization in Western India)*, Books & Books, New Delhi, 1995, p. 209.

[16]Dani and Masson, eds., op. cit., Chaps. 14 and 20.

people to be part of a Central Asian Bronze Age civilization.[17]

Intermediate homes and routes of the Proto-Indo-Aryans

It is not easy to locate the routes taken by the speakers of the Proto-Vedic language. The widely prevalent notion that the Vedic Indians and the Avestan Iranians lived together for a long time in Iran before the departure of the Indo-Aryans to India does not have adequate archaeological support. Evidence for the presence of the cults of fire and *soma* appears in Turkmenistan around the beginning of the second millennium BC, but not in the mainland of Iran. Probably the Proto-Indians and Proto-Iranians lived in Turkmenistan for some time.

Discussing the decline of the Bronze Age civilization and the movement of the tribes Masson states that unlike Turkmenistan and Transoxiana the sedentary farming communities did not bring new areas under cultivation in southern Afghanistan and south-eastern Iran.[18] He adds: 'For north-eastern Iran, where the outstanding Hissar-Turang-tepe culture flourished during the developed bronze period, no data are yet available to show what happened to the society after these large centres were depopulated at the beginning of the second millennium BC.'[19] The sudden collapse of the urban civilization in eastern Iran and in Afghanistan around 2000 BC is also underlined by Tosi and other archaeologists.[20] Further, they

[17]Fairservice, op. cit., in George Erdosy, ed., op. cit., pp. 210-11.

[18]Masson in Dani and Masson, eds., op. cit., p. 352.

[19]Ibid., pp. 351-2.

[20]M. Tosi, S. Malek Shahmirzadi and M.A. Joyenda, 'The Bronze Age in Iran and Afghanistan', in Dani and Masson, eds., op. cit., p. 215.

notice 'a radical and rapid decline of the large [urban] centres in all the enclaves of Central Asia' after 2200 BC.[21] The widespread urban decay may have increased the ranks of pastorals and agriculturists who looked for new lands because of climatic conditions and social conflicts. However, consequences of urban decay will be clear if more archaeological work is done on the second millennium BC.[22]

According to Harmatta the Proto-Iranian language was separated from the Proto-Indo-Aryan around 3500 BC. He adds that in the third millennium BC one group of the Proto-Indo-Aryans moved southward along the eastern coast of the Caspian Sea and conquered the Gorgan valley in north-eastern Iran where we find a large number of horse skeletons. Harmatta's decipherment of the names of Arisena and Somasena on an Agade inscription of *c.* 2300-2100 BC suggests that the Proto-Indo-Aryans had reached Mesopotamia via Iran. Ultimately they moved farther to the west and became a part of the Hurrian society in Mesopotamia. This accounts for the names of important 'Vedic' deities in Kassite inscriptions of *c.* 1600 BC.

Speaking of the movement of the eastern branch of the Indo-Europeans around 1500 BC, Ghirshman (1954) had suggested almost the same route of its migration to Mesopotamia as Harmatta (1992). According to him the warrior element in this branch moved eastward round the Caspian Sea, crossed the Caucasus and pushed to the great bend of the Euphrates. They settled among the local Harrians, and eventually founded the kingdom of Mitanni in north Mesopotamia and the valley of the northern Zagros.[23] In our view these were Proto-Indo-Aryans, whose

[21]Ibid., p. 200.

[22]Cf. ibid., p. 215.

[23]R. Ghirshman, *Iran From the Earliest Times to the Islamic Conquest*, Penguin, Harmondsworth, 1954, p. 61.

gods Indra, Varuṇa, Mitra and Nāsatya appear in the Mitanni inscription of the fourteenth century BC.

According to Burrow, the Proto-Indo-Aryans separated from the Proto-Iranians around 2000 BC. He implies that this separation took place outside Iran, and holds that instead of the Proto-Iranians the Proto-Indo-Aryans went first to Iran and settled in its eastern part in large numbers from where they migrated to India. In eastern Iran the Proto-Iranians appeared later and conquered it around 1400 BC. In our view the conquest may have compelled some Proto-Indo-Aryans to migrate to India. According to Burrow, the struggle between the Proto-Iranians and Proto-Indo-Aryans explains the hostility of the Iranians to the Indo-Aryan *devas* and their devotion to the Asura or Ahura. The *h*-speaking people eventually overpowered the *s*-speaking people in Iran.[24] Thus both Burrow and Harmatta agree that the Proto-Indo-Aryans separated from the Proto-Iranians outside Iran. They also agree that the Proto-Indo-Aryans went to Mesopotamia via Iran. Further, Ghirshman and Harmatta broadly agree on the migration route to Mesopotamia taken by the horsemen who worshipped 'Vedic' deities.

Burrow and Harmatta differ on the date of separation and also on the region from where the Proto-Indo-Aryans went to India. Harmatta places separation in 3500 BC while Burrow does it in 2000 BC. The Agade inscription cited by Harmatta suggests separation around 2500 BC. Further, Burrow thinks that the Proto-Indo-Aryans went from eastern Iran to India while Harmatta holds that they went from south Central Asia to India. However, in 1954 Ghirshman expressed a view similar to that of Harmatta.

[24]T. Burrow, 'The Proto-Indoaryans', *Journal of the Royal Asiatic Society*, 1973, pp. 123-40.

According to him, the bulk of the tribes, forming the eastern branch of the Indo-European movement, proceeded eastwards, crossed Transoxiana and the Oxus and had a short halt in the Bactrian plain. Then they crossed the passes in the Hindukush and adopted the classic route later followed by the invaders of India.[25] The view that the Proto-Indo-Aryans migrated from south Central Asia to India is better backed. Nevertheless, it is likely that some Proto-Indo-Aryans also went to India from Iran.

Harmatta states that the main bulk of Proto-Indians moved through Merv and Bactria, i.e. south Turkmenistan and north Afghanistan, to Gandhara and founded the Gandhara grave culture.[26] Archaeological evidence attests to the stay of the Proto-Indians in *c.* 1900-1500 BC in south Turkmenistan and north Afghanistan, from where they moved to Gandhara. Most probably they used Alexander's route. We may note that the Silk Road links Merv in south Turkmenistan with Bactra or Balkh in north Afghanistan from where it goes to Kabul, and from there to Peshawar in the Gandhara area. Once the Indo-Aryans appeared, gradually they spread their language over a wide area and asserted their presence in both India and Mesopotamia. However, the Proto-Indo-Aryans could not retain their language in Mesopotamia.

Textual references to immigration

Though direct references to the migrations of the Aryans into India are wanting, there is no dearth of indirect references and mythical traditions. It was because

[25] Ghirshman, op. cit., p. 63.

[26] J. Harmatta in Dani and Masson, eds., op. cit., pp. 371-5.

of this that Tilak postulated an outside home for the Aryans. Since the Aryans came through the mountains, which were considered the dwelling places of their gods, these are repeatedly mentioned in the *Ṛg Veda.* Meru, a mountain beyond the Himalaya, is a happy divine abode in the *Mahābhārata* and the Purāṇas.[27] The *Ṛg Veda* clearly suggests that the worshippers of the Maruts crossed the Sarayu (identical with the Avestan Harirud), the Indus and its four western tributaries and appeared on the east of the Indus. According to this text, neither the mountains nor the rivers hold up the Maruts, who are asked to cross Rasā, Anitabhā, Kubhā, Krumu, Sindhu and even the watery Sarayu for the sake of their votaries.[28] The *Ṛg Veda* also speaks of Indra winning stream after stream in favour of the Uśijs who, according to Geldner, were an ancient Aryan family. He adds that this reference implies the advance of the Aryans through the land of the five rivers.[29] According to the *Mahābhārata* myth, Śuka, son of Vyāsa, though capable of flying in the air, went to the earth on foot. 'He surmounted mighty rivers and lakes, passed through the mountains, reached even Meru, saw various lands, and that great muni came to the land of . . . Āryavarta.'[30] This myth may represent a tradition about Aryan immigration.

H.C. Raychaudhuri cites several Vedic and Purāṇic references which indicate that the Yadus, Turvasas, Kurus and Uttaramadras came to India from across the Himalayas.[31] The epic tales describe Purūravas Aila, one of

[27]E.A. Grantovsky and G.M. Bongard-Levin, *The Origin of Aryans from Scythia to India*, Arnold-Heinemann, New Delhi, 1980, pp. 46, 66.

[28]*ṚV,* V. 53.7 and 9.

[29]Ibid., I. 131.5; Karl Friedrich Geldner, *Harvard Oriental Series,* vol. 33, 1951, p. 185, fns. 5b and 5fg.

[30]Grantovsky and Bongard-Levin, op. cit., p. 70.

[31]Raychaudhuri, op. cit., pp. 23-4, 124-5, 140.

the earliest kings in Vedic texts, as the son of a ruler who migrated from Bahli or Bactria in the Oxus valley to mid-India.[32] As shown later, of the two sons of Purūravas from Urvaśī one is called the ancestor of the Kuru-Pañcālas and Kāśī-Videhas, and the other the ancestor of the Gandhāras, Pārśavas and Araṭṭas. The word Bālhika also occurs in the name of Prātipīya Bālhika, a Kuru king mentioned in the *Śatapatha Brāhmaṇa*.[33] This term was applied to Punjab when some people from Bactria came here. According to a tradition, the Kurus, who were the most important branch of the Ailas, were colonists from the trans-Himalayan region known as Uttarakuru.[34] A passage of the *Śatapatha Brāhmaṇa* shows that 'the speech of the Northerners—that is, presumably, the Northern Kurus . . . was regarded as specially pure'.[35] The *Kauṣītaki Brāhmaṇa* also speaks of the pure speech of the north.

It seems that the Uttarakurus did not have a complex society. The Śānti Parva states that in the land of the Uttarakurus the institution of marriage did not exist. According to the *Dīgha Nikāya*, in the land of Kuru 'men live calling no goods their own. Nor as their chattels any womenkind.'[36] These traditions suggest a simple society. Again, the two trans-Himalayan tribes, the Uttarakurus and Uttaramadras, are described in the *Aitareya Brāhmaṇa* as having a *vairājya* form of government.[37] *Vairājya* is interpreted by Kauṭilya as a kingless government in which people had no sense of thine and mine.[38] This implies that

[32]Ibid., p. 23 with fn. 17.
[33]Ibid., p. 23 with fn. 16.
[34]Ibid., p. 140.
[35]*Vedic Index*, I, p. 168.
[36]Sharma, *Aspects of Political Ideas and Institutions in Ancient India*, 1996, p. 50.
[37]*Aitareya Brāhmaṇa*, VIII. 14.
[38]*Arthaśāstra*, VIII. 2

these tribes had not developed the institution of the state and lived under the leadership of their chiefs. It seems that the state and complex society appeared when the immigrants had settled as full-fledged farmers in the Indian plains.

The latest study of the Ṛg Vedic history by Michael Witzel, a Sanskritist, gives convincing proof of migration. His analysis of the geographical data shows that Book 2 of the *Ṛg Veda* is clearly concerned with Afghanistan and the region west of the Indus while Books 4, 5, 6 and 8 either concentrate on the area west of the Indus or give considerable attention to it.[39] It may be added that the Ṛg Vedic area overlaps the Avestan area to a great extent. Both the texts cover Afghanistan, Pakistan and north-west India, though the Avesta includes north-eastern Iran and borders of south Central Asia. Witzel concludes that the mountainous country of Afghanistan is clearly the previous home of the Yadu-Turvas and Anu-Druhyu who appear as the earliest Aryan immigrants. The second wave of migration is represented by the Purus and the third by the Bharatas, a subtribe of the Purus. The *Jaiminīya Brāhmaṇa* remembers the crossing of the Sindhu by the incoming Bharatas and Ikṣvākus. More importantly, Witzel produces a passage from the *Baudhāyana Śrautasūtra*[40] which contains 'the most explicit statement of an immigration into the Subcontinent'.[41] This passage contains a dialogue between

[39]Michael Witzel, 'Rgvedic History: Poets, Chieftains and Polities', in George Erdosy, ed., op. cit., p. 317; cf. Nandi, op. cit., p. 10.

[40]*prāk ayu pravavrāja tasya ete kurupañcālāḥ kāśīvidehā etad āyavam, pravrajam pratyak amāvasuḥ tasya ete gāndhārayaḥ pārśavaḥ araṭṭāḥ iti etad amāvasam. The Baudhāyana Śrauta Sūtra Belonging to the Taittirīya Saṃhitā*, W. Caland, ed., vol. II, Asiatic Society, Calcutta, 1907, XVIII. 44.

[41]Witzel in George Erdosy, ed., op. cit., pp. 339-40.

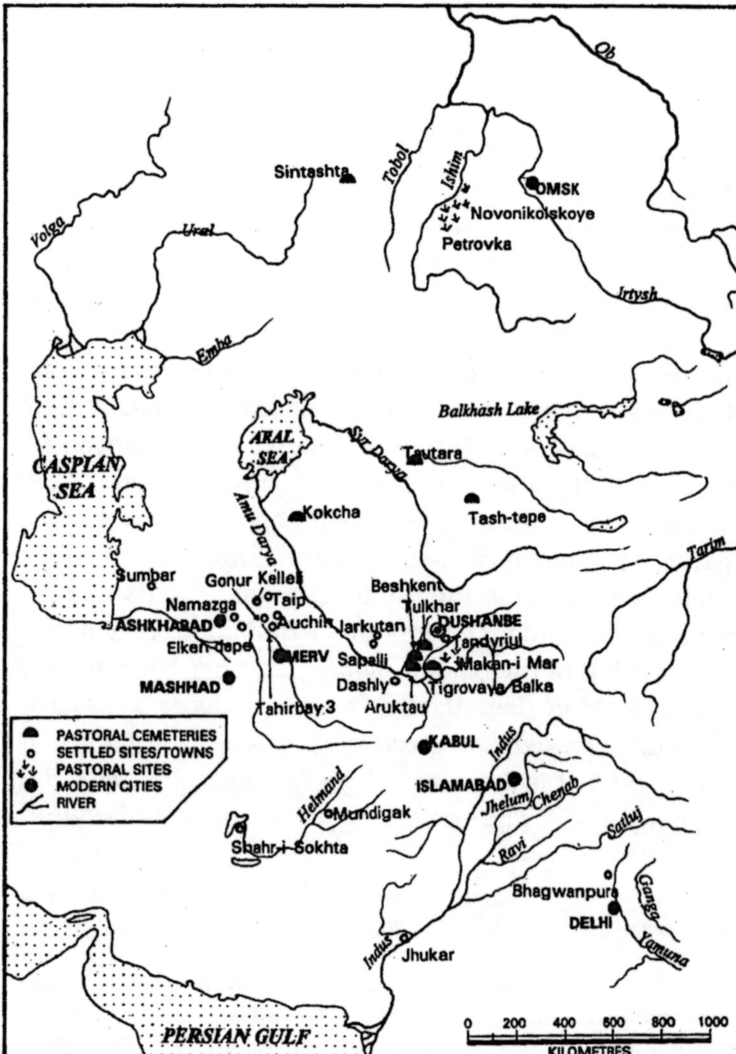

MAP 7: PASTORAL CEMETERIES AND OTHER RELATED SITES IN CENTRAL ASIA IN SECOND MILLENNIUM BC.

Aila Purūrava and Urvaśī, which refers to the horse, chariot parts, 100 houses and 100 jars of ghee. Towards the end it speaks of the birth of their sons Ayu and Amāvasu, who were asked by their mother to go out. 'Ayu went eastward. His people are the Kuru-Pañcālas and the Kāśī-Videhas. This is the Āyava kin group. Amāvasu stayed in the west. His people are the Gandharas, the Pārśavas and the Araṭṭas. This is the Amāvasava kin group.' The tribes mentioned here may have appeared and migrated much earlier, though the *Baudhāyana Śrautasūtra*, may not be earlier than the fifth century BC.[42] Perhaps members of the Amāvasava kin group used grey pottery and those of the Āyava kin group used Painted Grey Ware and Northern Black Polished Ware.[43] Possibly the former spoke the *r*- only dialect of the Indo-Aryan language in the north-west, and the latter spoke its *r*- and -*l* dialect in the eastern part of north India.[44]

Most probably Witzel's previous home for the earliest Ṛg Vedic tribes in Afghanistan is represented by the BMAC lying in south Turkmenistan, north Afghanistan and south Uzbekistan. Around 1500 BC settled oases in Margiana or south Turkmenistan show the domestic horse, models of chariots with spoked wheels, partial cremation and the svastika motif.[45] These traits may have emerged a couple of centuries earlier, for the Proto-Indo-Aryans appeared in this area around 1900 BC.[46] South Central Asia shows more than half a dozen graveyards which suggest movements of herdsmen. The archaeologists generally hold that these people moved from this area to the borders of the Indian subcontinent.

[42]Sukumari Bhattacharji, *Literature in the Vedic Age*, vol. 2, K.P. Bagchi & Co., Calcutta, 1986, p. 308; cf. ibid., pp. 318-19.

[43]Sharma, 1983, Appendix II.

[44]Deshpande in Erdosy, ed., op. cit., pp. 71-4.

[45]Masson in Dahi and Masson, eds., op. cit., p. 351.

[46]Parpola in Erdosy, ed., op. cit., p. 374.

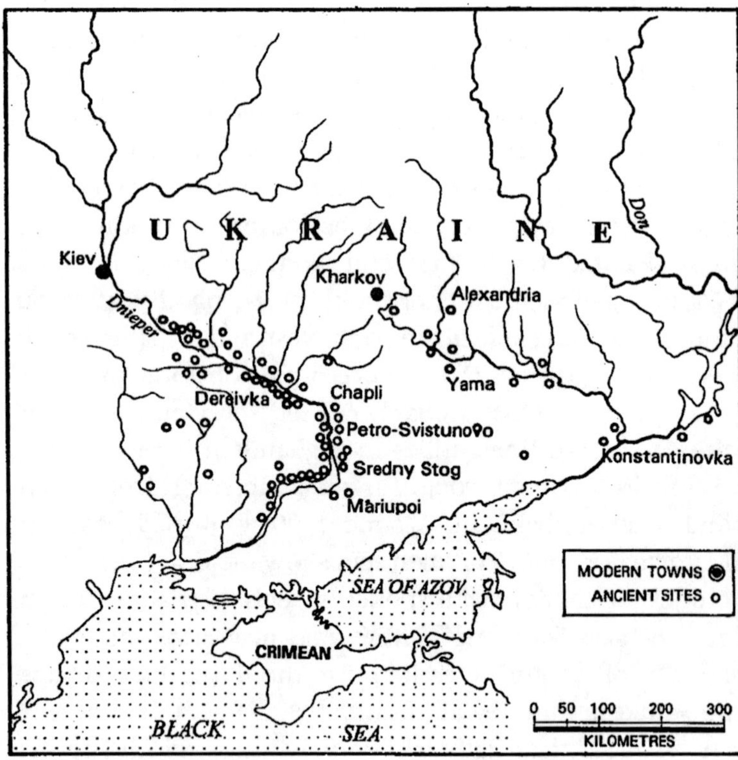

MAP 8: SREDNY STOG SITES 4500-3500 BC.

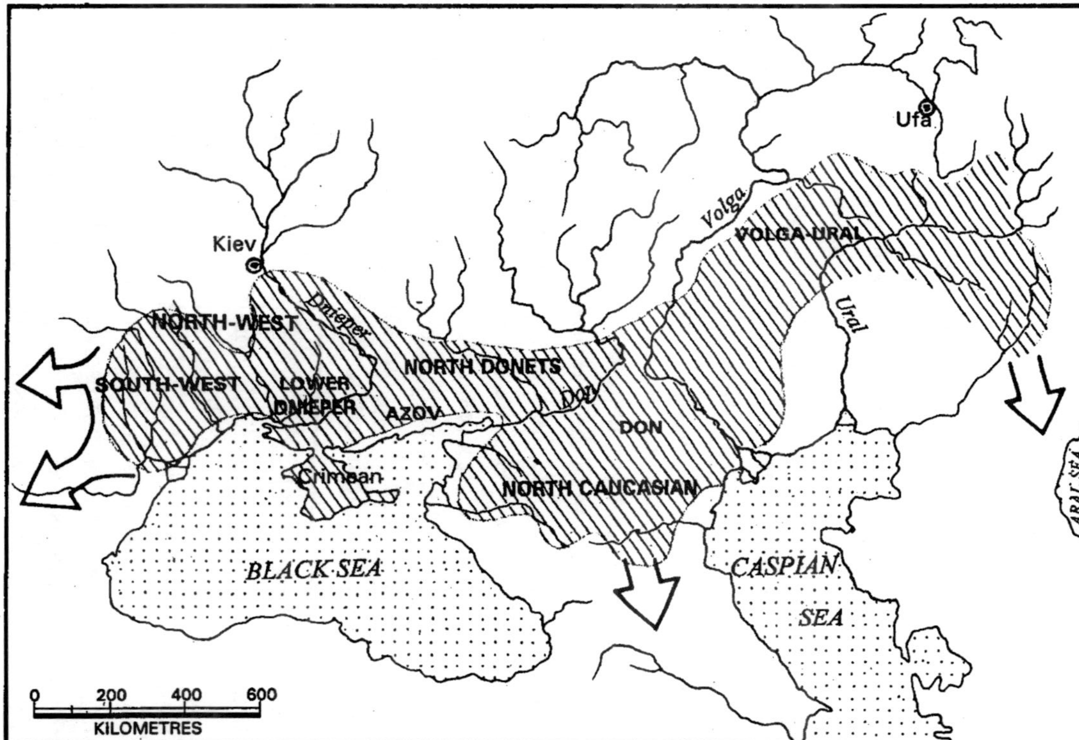

MAP 9: YAMNYA COMPLEX 3600-2200 BC.

Origin and crystallization of the Aryan culture

Where the Indo-European-speaking people, comprising the eastern and western branches, originated is difficult to say. A vast steppe area lying north of the Black Sea and the Caspian Sea extending from the Dnieper in the west to the Volga in the east is associated with horse-using tribes from the fifth millennium BC onwards. Gimbutas places them in the Volga area, marked by burials with surface structures called *kurgans*, but the Dnieper culture of horse-users appears to be older. Beginning with the Dnieper zone, following Mallory, we can mark three archaeological stages in the origin and expansion of the Indo-European or Aryan culture. The Sredny Stog complex in the steppe region of the Ukraine on the middle Dnieper in 4500-3500 BC marks the first stage. This complex shows the domestic horse used for riding and controlled by the use of antler cheek pieces. The people lived in houses which were slightly sunk in the ground. Thus we have beginnings of pit-dwelling, but surface houses were also in use. More pronounced features of the same culture appear in 3600-2200 BC in the Yamnya complex which extended from the Black Sea area in the west to the Volga-Ural region in the east. This complex marks the second important stage in the growth of the Indo-European culture in its spread towards Asia. It shows semi-subterranean houses in settlements and surface structures in burials. Apart from the increasing presence of the horse riders who used cheek pieces, we notice wagons and wheels together with more copper. We also find indications of animal sacrifices in burials.

The third important stage is provided by the Andronovo culture which practically covered the whole of

Central Asia in the second millennium BC. Most archaeologists who have worked in Central Asia see in this culture a counterpart of the culture reconstructed on the basis of elements common to the *Zend Avesta* and the *Ṛg Veda*. Archaeologically this culture gives considerable evidence of stockbreeding, wide use of horse, practice of cremation, pit-dwellings, constructed with birch and other types of wood, sacrifice altars and several other elements. We may specially mention the Sintashta culture which was one of the several variants of the Andronovo culture. Located on the Sintashta river in the south Urals adjoining the western border of Kazakhstan, around 1700 BC this culture comprised spoked wheels, war chariot, horse sacrifice and the use of the *soma* plant for drink. It is considered a counterpart of the Proto-Iranian culture, but it may also be called Indo-Aryan.

The fourth important stage in the spread of the Aryan culture can be postulated, following Parpola, in the Bactria-Margiana Complex of 1900-1500 BC. Lying in south Turkmenistan, north Afghanistan and also part of south Uzbekistan, this is considered to be a Proto-Indo-Aryan Complex from where the people migrated to the Indian borders and founded the Gandhara grave culture as well as other allied cultures.

The cultures of Eurasia mentioned earlier form a kind of sequence, but in terms of the time-scale an earlier culture may partly overlap with a later culture. Further, though all the four cultures are horse-using, their contents keep on changing in respect of the use and equipment of the horse, size of pit-dwelling along with the extent of birch wood in its construction, disposal of the dead, and various rituals.

Although the Andronovo and the Bactria-

Margiana Complex cultures represent the easterly branch of the Indo-European-speaking people, all those who moved into Asia did not speak the eastern branch of the Indo-European language. This seems to have been the case with the people of the Afanasievo culture which appeared on the Yeneisy around 3000 BC and continued up to 2000 BC. This culture is closely allied to the Yamnya culture of the Volga-Ural region and different from the Andronovo culture which appeared later and represented both Proto-Indian and Proto-Iranian elements. The Afanasievo culture is associated with the Tocharians who later moved about 1000 km south to the Tarim basin. It seems that these Tocharians eventually developed into the Indo-Iranians[47] and merged into them. The Tocharians came to India much later along with the Śakas and Kuṣāṇas. The ancient Indian texts place the Tukhāra land north-west of Madhyadeśa, and they also mention the Tukhāra horse. Since the Tocharians came from a cold zone the term *tuṣāra* used for the Tocharian in Sanskrit means cold or frigid.

How and when various tribal groups acquired the typical elements of the Proto-Indo-Iranian and Proto-Indo-Aryan cultures is difficult to find out. But there is little doubt that before the Proto-Indo-Aryans moved to the borderlands of the Indian subcontinent they stayed in the Sintashta region on the west of Kazakhstan, and probably a little later in south Turkmenistan and north Afghanistan. It seems likely that mixed groups of Proto-Indo-Aryans and Proto-Indo-Iranians lived together in the Sintastha region. We need data on the connection of this region with south Central Asia from where the Proto-Indo-Aryans moved to the border areas of the Indian subcontinent

[47] J.P. Mallory, *In Search of the Indo-Europeans*, pp. 223-6.

around 1500 BC. By this time they had picked up all the elements of the Aryan culture. The earliest specimens of their language appear in Western Asia, though it may have emerged in the fifth millennium BC or earlier. They seem to have used the horse in the same millennium in the Ukraine. They adopted the practice of cremation probably in Kazakhstan. The spoked wheel may have been the gift of the Caucasus area, and the war chariot assumed importance in the Sintashta region. Male domination can be traced in the fourth millennium BC in the middle Dnieper culture in the Ukraine; in the second millennium BC men were placed on the right and women on the left in many pastoralist graves in Central Asia. The fire cult appears in the form of hearths in the Ukraine. Around 1400 BC and later such hearths reach south Tajikistan and develop into the Vedic form of the householder's fire (*gārhapatya*) and sacrificial fire cult (*āhavanīya*). Animal sacrifice also appears in the earlier cultures in the Black Sea region and continues later in Central Asian cultures. Pastoralism is common to all steppe cultures and along with a common language it may have unified Aryan communities. But it does not exclude agriculture. In the north Indian plains the Indo-Aryans become full-fledged agriculturists. The *Ṛg Veda* contains agricultural terms which have no cognates in other Indo-European languages. It seems that the svastika motif travelled from the area of Elam to Baluchistan and Central Asia.

We learn that the Huns were an amalgam of Turkic, Iranian and Germanic-speaking peoples.[48] They may have been a mixed people. Although the Indo-Aryans spoke a language similar to the Iranians, they appear to be

[48]Mallory, op. cit., p. 61.

a mixed ethnic group who brought to India a new language and a composite culture. Whatever be the origin of the term *ārya*, for sometimes it is regarded as a non-Indo-European term borrowed from Western Asia,[49] it came into general usage in Iran and India, and eventually the Aryans came to be regarded as an integrated community dominated by the users of the horse and chariot. It seems that the Indo-Aryans, who came to India under their chiefs, initially constituted a composite cultural community with a strong presence of kin-based subgroups. The earliest Vedic chiefdom, though horse-centred, seems to have been a simple organization which was yet to develop social stratification and complicated rituals.

Post-Vedic migrations and invasions

The Proto-Indo-Aryans did not have to look for routes to the Indian subcontinent, for the Harappans had crossed the high passes of the Hindukush and reached the middle course of the Amu Darya where they had set up a trading post at Shortugai. Even in post-Vedic centuries the speakers of the Indo-European language continued to come to India through Khaibar, Bolan, Gomal and several other passes as invaders or immigrants. In 517 BC the Achaemenids occupied the north-west part. In 326 BC the Macedonian Greeks invaded India under Alexander. In 205 BC the Bactrian Greeks raided the north-west. In the second and the first centuries BC the Śakas, Pahlavas and the Kuṣāṇas continued their inroads into India. With them came the Tocharians, who were originally speakers of the western branch of the Indo-European language but were later transformed into an Indo-Iranian-speaking people.

[49]Ibid., p. 276, fn. 27.

The Huns appeared in the fifth century AD. Thus we have solid historical evidence to show that people kept on moving from Central Asia to India for about one thousand years. If this could happen in post-Vedic centuries, could it not be possible in Vedic times?

Yet, it was not always a one-way traffic. The Harappans had set up a colony in Afghanistan, and their influence in Turkmenistan can be clearly seen in various ceramic and metal objects from Altyn-depe.[50] After the spread of the speakers of the Indo-Aryan language in north India Buddhist missionaries went to Afghanistan and Central Asia where they preached their religion. Apparently they were helped by linguistic affinities.

[50]Masson in Dani and Masson, eds., op. cit., 242.

Summing up

The bearers of the Aryan culture were basically kin-based cattle-rearers dominated by horsemen and war charioteers. They practised cremation and animal sacrifice, drank *soma* and worshipped fire. They lived in pits covered with various types of wood including the birch. Their society was male-dominated. These traits of the Aryan culture are attested archaeologically in the second millennium BC in Central Asia.

The Aryans of Central Asia, especially of the south, may have been in contact with the Harappan culture towards the end of its urban phase. But the Harappan culture cannot be called Aryan or Vedic. Important elements of the Aryan culture appear in the archaeology of south Central Asia in 1900-1500 BC, though the earliest inscriptional specimens of its language are found in Western Asia in *c.* 2300 BC.

In the Indian subcontinent the archaeological counterpart of the early Vedic culture appears not in Harappa but in the borderland cultures of the Swat valley, Gomal valley and the Pirak complex and perhaps in Periano Ghundai. It emerges clearly in south Central Asia in the Bactria-Margiana Archaeological Complex and in the culture of south Tajikistan. Though the post-Harappan cultures in north India may have adopted indigenous elements, they were fundamentally different from the Harappan culture. Their emergence on the borderlands suggests immigration from outside. This is supported by indirect references in the *Ṛg Veda* whose several books either concentrate on the area lying west of the Indus or give enough attention to it. Some later Vedic texts clearly speak of migration from the west. Further, many myths and traditions, particularly about Āryāvarta, Bālhika, Himavanta, Meru, Uttarakuru and Uttaramadra, in later Vedic texts, early Pali texts and in the epics and the Purāṇas, suggest immigration.

The Indo-Aryan language was spread by the horse-using people who came from south Central Asia. It gradually replaced the Dravidian language which was spoken earlier in a major part of the subcontinent. This explains the presence of the Dravidian substratum in the Indo-Aryan languages, though words of Munda stock are not entirely absent in them.

The view that the Indo-Aryans came to India from outside is not acceptable to Hindu fundamentalists and the western champions of the continuity of the local cultural tradition. The implications of the fundamentalist position are well known in India and even abroad. But those of the theory of the continuity of the cultural tradition need consideration. Formerly some Western historians and sociologists stressed the changelessness of India, and archaeologists like Spooner and Wheeler attributed important changes to external factors. Now some archaeologists emphasize India's insularity, which implies its inability to attract new peoples and technology. Some of them rightly reject the view that the Harappan civilization was

Aryan or Ṛg Vedic.[1] But several of them see in the advent of the Vedic culture a continuity of the Harappan or the chalcolithic tradition rather than a phase of breakthrough and transformation. Their exaggeration of cultural continuity may be seen as a reaction to overemphasis on a plea for a radical change in the modern socio-economic structure.

All this reminds us of the eternal or *sanātana* dharma propagated in present times. A purely localistic continuity approach neither advances archaeological understanding nor helps historical reconstruction. It is necessary to assess the relative importance of change and continuity in the context of time and place. More importantly, we need to differentiate between radical and peripheral changes, and explain the relative role of both internal and external agents in making them. Text-aided archaeology and archaeology-aided text combined with linguistic studies should prove useful in this exercise.

[1]Jim G. Shaffer, 'The Indo-Aryan Invasions: Cultural Myth and Archaeological Reality', in John R. Luckas, ed., *The People of South Asia*, Plenum Press, New York and London, 1984, Chap. 4; Erdosy, in Jonathan Mark Kenoyer, ed., *Contributions to the Archaeology of South and East Asia*, Wisconsin Archaeological Reports, vol. 3, Madison, 1994, p. 224.

Bibliography

Andronov, M.S., *Dravidian Languages*, 'Nauka' Publishing House, Moscow, 1970.

————, *The Brahui Language*, 'Nauka' Publishing House, Moscow, 1980.

Agrawal, D.P. and A. Ghosh, eds., *Radiocarbon and Indian Archaeology*, Tata Institute of Fundamental Research, Bombay, 1973.

Agrawal, D.P., 'Metals (Technology)', in A. Ghosh, ed., *An Encyclopaedia of Indian Archaeology*, vol. I, Munshiram Manoharlal, New Delhi, 1989, pp. 324-5.

Aitareya Brāhmaṇa with commentary of Sāyaṇa, ed. T. Weber, Bonn, 1879.

Allchin, Bridget and Raymond Allchin, *The Birth of Indian Civilization,* Penguin, Harmondsworth, 1968.

————, *Origins of a Civilization, The Prehistory and Early Archaeology of South Asia,* Viking, Penguin Books India, New Delhi, 1997.

Anthony, David W., 'The "Kurgan Culture", Indo-European origins and the domestication of the horse: A reconsideration', in *Current Anthropology*, vol. 27, no. 4, Aug.-Oct. 1986, pp. 291-313.

————, 'Migration in Archaeology: The Baby and Bathwater', *American Anthropologist,* vol. 92, no. 4, 1990, pp. 895-914.

Anthony, David W. and Bernard Wailes, Review of C. Renfrew's *Archaeology and Language: The Puzzle of Indo-European Origins*, in *Current Anthropology*, vol. 29, no. 3, June 1988, pp. 441-5.

Askarov, A., V. Volkov and N. Ser-Odjav, 'Pastoral and nomadic tribes at the beginning of the first millennium B.C.', in A.H. Dani and V.M. Masson, eds., *History of Civilizations of Central Asia*, vol. I, UNESCO Publishing, Paris, 1992, pp. 459-72.

Banerji, A., 'Banawali', in A. Ghosh, ed., *An Encyclopaedia of Indian Archaeology*, vol. II, Munshiram Manoharlal, New Delhi, 1989, pp. 45-6.

Bhan, Suraj, 'The Sequence and Spread of Prehistoric Cultures in the upper Sarasvati Basin', in D.P. Agrawal and A. Ghosh, eds., *Radiocarbon and Indian Archaelogy*, Tata Institute of Fundamental Research, Bombay, 1973, pp. 252-63.

————, *Excavation at Mitathal (1968) and Other Explorations in the Sutlej-Yamuna Divide*, Kurukshetra University, Kurukshetra, 1975.

Bhattacharji, Sukumari, *Literature in the Vedic Age*, vol. 2, The Brahmaṇas, Āraṇyakas, Upaniṣads and Sūtras, K.P. Bagchi & Company, Calcutta, 1986.

Bisht, R.S., 'Excavations at Banawali: 1974-77', in Gregory L. Possehl, ed., *Harappan Civilization: A Contemporary Perspective*, Oxford and IBH, New Delhi, 1982, pp. 113-39.

Biswas, A.K., 'The Aryan Myth', in A. Ray and S. Mukherji, eds., *Historical Archaeology*, Books & Books, New Delhi, 1990, pp. 29-49.

Bose, D.M., S.N. Sen and B.V. Subbrayappa, eds., *A Concise History of Science in India*, National Science Academy, New Delhi, 1971.

Burrow, T., *The Sanskrit Language*, Faber and Faber, London, 1955.

————, 'The Proto-Indoaryans', *Journal of the Royal Asiatic Society*, 1973, pp. 123-40.

Caland, W., ed., *The Baudhāyana Śrauta Sūtra Belonging to the Taittirīya Saṃhitā*, vol. II, Asiatic Society, Calcutta, 1907.

Dani, A.H. and V.M. Masson, eds., *History of Civilizations of Central Asia*, vol. I, UNESCO Publishing, Paris, 1992.

Dani, A.H., 'Pastoral-agricultural tribes of Pakistan in the Post-

Indus period', in A.H. Dani and V.M. Masson, eds., *History of Civilizations of Central Asia*, vol. I, UNESCO Publishing, Paris, 1992, pp. 395-420.

Desai, D., 'Animal (Terracotta Figurines)', in A. Ghosh, ed., *An Encyclopaedia of Indian Archaeology*, vol. I, Munshiram Manoharlal, New Delhi, 1989, pp. 338-9.

Deshpande, Madhav M. and Peter Edwin Hook, eds., *Aryan and Non-Aryan in India*, University of Michigan Press, Ann Arbor, 1979.

Dhavalikar, M.K., *Cultural Imperialism (Indus Civilization in Western India)*, Books & Books, New Delhi, 1995.

Diakonov, I.M., 'On the Original home of the speakers of Indo-European', *Journal of Indo-European Studies*, vol. 13, 1985, pp. 92-174.

Ehrich, Robert W., ed., *Chronologies in Old World Archaeology*, vol. I, 3rd edn, University of Chicago Press, Chicago, 1992.

Erdosy, George, 'The meaning of Ṛgvedic *pur*: Notes on the Vedic landscape', in Jonathan Mark Kenoyer, ed., *From Sumer to Meluha: Contributions to the Archaeology of South and East Asia in Memory of George F. Dales, Jr.*, Wisconsin Archaeological Reports, vol. 3, Madison, 1994, pp. 223-34.

Erdosy, George, ed., *The Indo-Aryans of Ancient South Asia: Language, Material culture and Ethnicity*, Walter de Gruyter and Co., Berlin, 1995; 1st Indian edn, Munshiram Manoharlal, New Delhi, 1997.

Fairservice (Jr.), Walter A., 'Central Asia and the Ṛgveda: The archaeological evidence', in George Erdosy, ed., *The Indo-Aryans of Ancient South Asia*, Munshiram Manoharlal, New Delhi, 1997, pp. 206-12.

Frankfort, Henri-Paul, 'New data illustrating the early contacts between Central Asia and the North West of the Sub-Continent', in Catherine Jarrige, ed., *South Asian Archaeology*, 1989, Prehistory Press, Madison, 1992, pp. 97-102.

Gamkrelidge, T.V. and V.V. Ivanov, 'The Migrations of Tribes Speaking the Indo-Aryan Dialects from their Original

Home in the Near East to their Historical Habitations in Eurasia', *Journal of Indo-European Studies,* vol. 13, nos. 1 and 2, 1985, pp. 49-91.

———, *Indo-European and the Indo-Europeans,* pt I, The Text, Mouton de Gruyter, New York, 1995.

Gening, V.F., 'The Cemetry at Sintashta and the Early Indo-Iranian Peoples', *Journal of Indo-European Studies,* vol. 7, nos. 3 and 4, 1979, pp. 1-29.

Ghirshman, R., *Iran From the Earliest Times to the Islamic Conquest,* Penguin, Harmondsworth, 1954.

Gimbutas, Marija, 'Primary and Secondary Homeland of the Indo-European: Comment on Gamkrelidge and Ivanov Article', *JIES,* vol. 13, 1985, nos. 1 and 2, pp. 185-202.

Ghosh, A., ed., *An Encyclopaedia of Indian Archaeology,* 2 vols., Munshiram Manoharlal, New Delhi, 1989.

Gordon, Kent H. and Kenneth L. Pike, 'Paired Semantic Components, Paired Sentence Reversals and the Analysis of Dhāṅgar-Kudux Discourse', in Ronald L. Trail, *Patterns in Clause, Sentence and Discourse in selected Languages of India and Nepal,* pt I, Sentence and Discourse, Summer Institute of Linguistics of the University of Okalahama, Norman, U.S.A., 1973.

Grantovsky, E.A. and G.M. Bongard-Levin, *The Origin of Aryans from Scythia to India,* Arnold-Heinemann, New Delhi, 1980.

Gupta, S.P., ed., *The 'Lost' Sarasvati and the Indus Civilization,* Kusumanjali Publishers, Jodhpur, 1995.

———, 'The Indus-Saraswati Civilization: Some New Developments', in S.P. Gupta, ed., *The 'Lost' Sarasvati and the Indus Civilization,* Kusumanjali Publishers, Jodhpur, 1995, pp. 180-200.

Harmatta, J., 'The emergence of the Indo-Iranian languages', in A.H. Dani and V.M. Masson, eds., *History of Civilizations of Central Asia,* vol. I, UNESCO Publishing, Paris, 1992, pp. 357-78.

Hiebert, Fredrik T., 'South Asia from a Central Asian perspective', in George Erdosy, ed., *The Indo-Aryans of Ancient South Asia,* Munshiram Manoharlal, New Delhi, 1997, pp. 192-205.

The Iliad of Homer, tr. E.V. Rieu, Penguin, Harmondsworth, rpt, 1986.

Indian Archaeology 1961-62: A Review, Archaeological Survey of India, New Delhi, 1968.

Kachru, Braj, 'Kashmiri and other Dardic Languages', in Norman H. Zide, ed., *Current Trends in Linguistics*, vol. V, *Linguistics in South Asia*, Mouton, The Hague, 1969, pp. 284-306.

Joshi, J.P., *Excavation at Bhagwanpura: 1975-1976*, ASI, Govt. of India, New Delhi, 1993.

The Kauṭilya Arthaśāstra, ed., and tr. R.P. Kangle, 3 pts, University of Bombay, 1960-5.

Kennedy, Kenneth A.R., 'Have Aryans been identified in the prehistoric skeletal record from South Asia? Biological anthropology and the concepts of ancient races', in George Erdosy, ed., *The Indo-Aryans of Ancient South Asia*, Munshiram Manoharlal, New Delhi, 1997, pp. 32-66.

Kenoyer, J.M., ed., *Old Problems and New Perspective of the Archaeology of South Aisa*, Wisconsin Archaeological Reports, vol. 2, Madison, 1989.

————, ed., *From Sumer to Meluha: Contributions to the Archaeology of South and East Asia in Memory of George F. Dales, Jr.*, Wisconsin Archaeological Reports, vol. 3, Madison, 1994.

————, 'Interaction systems, specialised crafts and culture change: The Indus Valley Tradition and the Indo-Gangetic Tradition in South Asia', in George Erdosy, ed., *The Indo-Aryans of Ancient South Asia*, Munshiram Manoharlal, New Delhi, 1997, pp. 213-57.

Kumar, Mrityunjay, 'The Puruṣamedha and Aśvamedha: An Historical Study', Ph.D. Thesis, University of Delhi, 1998.

Kuzmina, Y.Y. and K.F. Smirnov, 'The Origin of the Indo-Iranians in the Light of Recent Archaeological Data', *Journal of Central Asia*, vol. I, no. 1, 1978, pp. 68-70.

Lal, B.B., *The Earliest Civilization of South Asia*, Aryan Books International, New Delhi, 1997.

————, 'The Indo-Aryan Hypothesis *vis-a-vis* Indian Archaeology', *Journal of Central Asia*, vol. I, no. 1, July 1978, pp. 21-41.

————, 'Some reflections on the structural remains at Kalibanga', in B.B. Lal and S.P. Gupta, eds., *Frontiers of the Indus Civilization*, Books & Books, New Delhi, 1984, pp. 55-62.

————, 'Painted Grey Ware (PGW)', in A. Ghosh, ed., *An Encyclopaedia of Indian Archaeology*, vol. I, Munshiram Manoharlal, New Delhi, 1989, pp. 107-8.

————, 'The Painted Grey Ware Culture of the Iron Age', in A.H. Dani and V.M. Masson, eds., *History of Civilizations of Central Asia*, UNESCO Publishing, Paris, 1992, pp. 421-40.

Lal, B.B. and S.P. Gupta, eds., *Frontiers of the Indus Civilization*, Books & Books, New Delhi, 1984.

Litvinsky, B.A. and L.T. Pyankova, 'Pastoral tribes of the Bronze Age in the Oxus Valley (Bactria)', in A.H. Dani and V.M. Masson, eds., *History of Civilizations of Central Asia*, vol. I, UNESCO Publishing, Paris, 1992, pp. 379-94.

Luckas, John R., ed., *The People of South Asia*, Plenum Press, New York and London, 1984.

Macdonell, A.A. and A.B. Keith, *Vedic Index of Names and Subjects*, vol. I, Motilal Banarsidass, Delhi, 3rd rpt, 1967.

Mackay, Ernest, *Early Indus Civilization*, Clay and Sons, London, 1935; 2nd enlarged and revd edn, edited by D. Mackay, Luzac, London, 1948 and Indological Book Corporation, Delhi, 1976.

Mallory, J.P., *In Search of the Indo-Europeans Language, Archaeology and Myth*, Thames and Hudson, paperback edn, London, 1991.

————, 'Migration and Language Change', in *Universitetets Oldsaksamlings Skrifter Ny rekke, Nr. 14, Peregrinatio Gothica III*, Fredrikstad, Norway, 1991, Oslo, 1992, pp. 145-53.

Manik, S. and S.A. Chanchal, *The Aryans and the Indus Civilization*, Dinratri Prakashan, Dhaka, 1995.

Masica, Colin P., 'Aryan and Non-Aryan Elements in North Indian Agriculture', in M. Deshpande and Peter Edwin Hook, ed., *Aryan and Non-Aryan in India*, University of Michigan Press, Ann Arbor, 1979, pp. 55-151.

Masson, V.M., 'The Bronze Age in Khorasan and Transoxania',

in A.H. Dani and V.M. Masson, eds., *History of Civilizations of Central Asia*, vol. I, UNESCO Publishing, Paris, 1992, pp. 225-46.

————, 'The decline of the Bronze Age Civilization and movements of the tribes', in A.H. Dani and V.M. Masson, eds., *History of Civilizations of Central Asia,* vol. I, UNESCO Publishing, Paris, 1992, pp. 337-56.

Max Müller, F., *Biographies of Words and the Home of the Aryans,* Longman, Green, London, 1888.

McAlpin, David W., 'Linguistic Prehistory: The Dravidian Situation', in Madhav M. Deshpande and Peter Edwin Hook, eds., *Aryan and Non-Aryan in India,* University of Michigan Press, Ann Arbor, 1979, pp. 175-88.

Meadow, Richard, 'Continuity and Change in the agriculture of the Great Indus Valley: The palaeoethnobotanical and zooarchaeological evidence', in J.M. Kenoyer, ed., *Old Problems and New Perspective of the Archaeology of South Asia,* Wisconsin Archaeological Reports, vol. 2, Madison, 1989, pp. 61-74.

Misra, V.D., 'Origin and Antiquity of the Painted Grey Ware', *University of Allahabad Studies,* vol. 2 (n.s.), no. 1, January 1970, pp. 11-24.

Mongait, Alexander, *Archaeology in the U.S.S.R.*, Foreign Languages Publishing House, Moscow, 1959.

Monier-Williams, M., *A Sanskrit English Dictionary,* Oxford University Press, rpt, Motilal Banarsidass, Delhi, 1986.

Mughal, M. Rafique, 'Recent Archaeological Research in the Cholistan Desert', in Gregory L. Possehl, ed., *Harappan Civilization: A Contemporary Perspective,* Oxford and IBH, New Delhi, 1982, pp. 107-24.

Nandi, R.N., 'Aryan Settlements and the Ṛgveda', *Indian Historical Review,* vol. XXI, nos. 1 and 2, July 1994/January 1995, pp. 9-36.

Nyberg, Harri, 'The problem of the Aryans and the Soma: The botanical evidence', in George Erdosy, ed., *The Indo-Aryans of Ancient South Asia,* Munshiram Manoharlal, New Delhi, 1997, pp. 382-406.

The Odyssey of Homer, tr. E.V. Rieu, rpt, Penguin, Harmondsworth, 1986.

Parpola, Asko, 'The Problem of the Aryans and the Soma: Textual-linguistic and archaeological evidence', in George Erdosy, ed., *The Indo-Aryans of Ancient South Asia*, Munshiram Manoharlal, New Delhi, 1997, pp. 353-81.

————, 'The Coming of the Aryans to Iran and India and the Cultural and Ethnic Identity of the Dāsas', *International Journal of Dravidian Linguistics*, XVII, no. 2, pp. 85-228.

Possehl, Gregory L., ed., *Harappan Civilization: A Contemporary Perspective*, Oxford and IBH, New Delhi, 1982.

Possehl, Gregory L., 'Radiocarbon Dates for South Asian Archaeology', University Museum, University of Pennsylvania, Philadelphia, June 1989 (cyclostyled copy).

Raichaudhury, H.C., *Political History of Ancient India*, 7th edn, University of Calcutta, Calcutta, 1972.

Rao, S.R., *Lothal and the Indus Civilization*, Asia Publishing House, Bombay, 1973.

————, *Lothal: A Harappan Port Town*, Memoirs of the Archaeological Survey of India, no. 78, New Delhi, 1979.

————, 'New Light on the Post-Urban (Late Harappan) Phase of the Indus Civilization in India', in Gregory L. Possehl, ed., *Harappan Civilization: A Contemporary Perspective*, New Delhi, 1982, pp. 353-9.

Rau, Wilhelm, *The Meaning of pur in Vedic Literature*, Wilhelm Fink Verlag, Munchen, 1976.

Renfrew, C., *Archaeology and Language: The Puzzle of Indo-European Origins*, Penguin, Harmondsworth, 1989.

Ṛgveda Saṃhitā with the commentary of Sāyaṇa, 5 vols., Vaidik Samshodhan Mandal, Pune, 1933-5. *Ṛg-Veda-Saṃhita*, vol. III, ed. F. Max Müller, Oxford University Press, 1892. Tr. of the first six Mandalas, H.H. Wilson, London, 1850-7. Tr. under the title *The Hymns of the Ṛgveda* by Ralph T.H. Griffith, rpt, Motilal Banarsidass, Delhi, 1986. Tr. in German by K.F. Geldner named *Der Rigveda aus dem Sanskrit in Dutsch ubersetzt*, Harvard Oriental Series, nos. 33-5, Harvard University Press, Cambridge, Massachusetts, 1951-7.

Saha, M.N. and N.C. Lahiri, *History of the Calenders*, Council of Scientific and Industrial Research, New Delhi, 1955, rpt, 1992.

Sankalia, H.D., *Prehistory and Protohistory of India and Pakistan*, Deccan College Postgraduate and Research Institute, Pune, 1974.

Sarianidi, V.I., 'Ancient Bactria: New Aspects of An Old Problem', in *Journal of Central Asia*, vol. I, no. 1, July 1978, pp. 76-7.

Sethna, K.D., *The Problem of Aryan Origin from an Indian Perspective*, S. & S. Publishers, Calcutta, 1980.

Shaffer, Jim G., 'The Indo-Aryan Invasions: Cultural Myth and Archaeological Reality', in John R. Luckas, ed., *The People of South Asia*, Plenum Press, New York and London, 1984, pp. 77-90.

——————, 'The Indus Valley, Baluchistan and Helmand Traditions: Neolithic through Bronze Age', in Robert W. Ehrich, ed., *Chronologies in Old World Archaeology*, vol. I, 3rd edn, University of Chicago Press, Chicago, 1992, pp. 441-64.

Shaffer, Jim G. and B.K. Thapar, 'Pre-Indus and early Indus cultures of Pakistan and India', in A.H. Dani and V.M. Masson, eds., *History of Civilizations of Central Asia*, vol. I, UNESCO Publishing, Paris, 1992, pp. 247-82.

Sharif, M. and B.K. Thapar, 'Food-producing communities in Pakistan and northern India', in A.H. Dani and V.M. Masson, eds., *History of Civilizations of Central Asia*, vol. I, UNESCO Publishing, Paris, 1992, pp. 127-51.

Sharma, R.S., *Urban Decay in India (c. 300-c. 1000)*, Munshiram Manoharlal, New Delhi, 1987.

——————, *Śūdras in Ancient India*, 3rd edn, Motilal Banarsidass, Delhi, 1990.

——————, *Material Culture and Social Formations in Ancient India*, Macmillan, Delhi, 1997.

——————, *Looking for the Aryans*, Orient Longman, Chennai, 1994.

——————, *Aspects of Political Ideas and Institutions in Ancient India*, 4th edn, Motilal Banarsidass, Delhi, 1996.

——————, *The State and Varna Formation in the Mid-Ganga Plains: An Ethnoarchaeological View*, Manohar, New Delhi, 1996.

——————, Review of L. Kohl and Clare Fawcett, eds., *Nationalism, Politics and the Practice of Archaeology*,

Cambridge University Press, Bentley House, London, 1995, *Newsletter of Archaeology, Anthropology, History, South Asia Network*, Issue 5/Summer 1997, pp. 17-18.

Singh, Sarva Daman, *Ancient Indian Warfare with Special Reference to the Vedic Period*, E.J. Brill, Leiden, 1965.

Smith, Morton, 'What is in a name (in ancient India)?', *Journal of Indo-European Studies*, 12, 1984, pp. 293-313.

Southworth, Franklin C., 'Lexical Evidence for Early Contacts between Indo-Aryan and Dravidian', in Madhav M. Deshpande and Peter Edwin Hook, eds., *Aryan and Non-Aryan in India*, University of Michigan Press, Ann Arbor, 1979, pp. 191-233.

————, 'Reconstructing Social Context from Language: Indo-Aryan and Dravidian Prehistory', in George Erdosy, ed., *The Indo-Aryans of Ancient South Asia*, Munshiram Manoharlal, New Delhi, 1997, pp. 258-77.

Srivastava, K.M., 'The Myth of Aryan Invasion of Harappan Towns', in B.B. Lal and S.P. Gupta, eds., *Frontiers of the Indus Civilization*, Books & Books, New Delhi, 1984, pp. 437-43.

Stacul, Giorgio, 'Harappan Post-urban Evidence in the Swat Valley', in B.B. Lal and S.P. Gupta, eds., *Frontiers of the Indus Civilization*, Books & Books, New Delhi, 1984, pp. 271-5.

————, *Prehistoric and Protohistoric Swat, Pakistan (c. 3000-1400 BC)*, Rome, ISMEO, 1987.

Subbarayappa, B.V., *Indus Script: Its Nature and Structure*, New Era Publications, Chennai, 1996.

Thapar, Romila, 'The Theory of Aryan Race and India: History and Politics', *Transactions of the International Conference of Eastern Studies*, no. XL, 1995, pp. 41-66.

Tosi, M., S. Malek Shahmirzadi and M.A. Joyenda, 'The Bronze Age in Iran and Afghanisatn', in A.H. Dani and V.M. Masson, eds., *History of Civilizations of Central Asia*, vol. I, UNESCO Publishing, Paris, 1992, pp. 191-224.

Trautmann, Thomas R., 'The Study of Dravidian Kinship', in Madhav M. Deshpande and Peter Edwin Hook, eds., *Aryan and Non-Aryan in India*, Unversity of Michigan Press, Ann Arbor, 1979, pp. 153-73.

———, *Aryans and British India*, Vistaar Publication, New Delhi, 1997.

Tripathi, Vibha, *The Painted Grey Ware: An Iron Age Culture of Northern India*, Concept Publishing, Delhi, 1976.

Turner, R.L., *A Comparative Dictionary of the Indo-Aryan Languages*, Oxford University Press, London, 1966.

Unger-Hamilton, Romana, 'The Epi-Palaeolithic Southern Levant and the Origins of Cultivation', *Current Anthropology*, vol. 30, no. 1, Feb. 1989, pp. 88ff.

Vats, M.S., *Excavations at Harappa*, 2 vols., Government of India, Delhi, 1940.

Verma, Ramchandra, ed., *Saṃkṣhipta Hindi Śabdasāgara*, Nagaripracharini Sabha, Kashi, 1987.

Wheeler, R.E.M., *The Indus Civilization*, 3rd edn, Cambridge University Press, Bentley House, London, 1968.

Witzel, Michael, 'Ṛgvedic History: Poets, Chieftains and Polities', in George Erdosy, ed., *The Indo-Aryans of Ancient South Asia*, Munshiram Manoharlal, New Delhi, 1997, pp. 307-56.

Wojtilla, Gy., 'The Sanskrit Terminology of the Plough', *Acta Orientalia Academiae Scientiarum Hung Tomus*, XLII, nos. 2-3, 1988, pp. 325-38.

The Zend Avesta, pt I, The Vendidad, tr. James Darmesteter, *SBE*, vol. IV, rpt, Motilal Banarsidass, Delhi, 1992; pt II, tr. James Darmesteter, *SBE*, vol. XXIII, rpt, Motilal Banarsidass, Delhi, 1988; Pt. III, tr. L.H. Mills, *SBE*, vol. XXXI, rpt, Motilal Banarsidass, Delhi, 1988.

Zide, Norman H., ed., *Current Trends in Linguistics*, vol. V, *Linguistics in South Asia*, Mouton, The Hague, 1969.

Zvelebil, M. and K.V. Zvelebil, 'Agricultural transition and Indo-European dispersals', *Antiquity*, vol. 62, no. 236, Sept. 1988, pp. 574-83.

Index